A Soldier's Silent Prayer

Sherry Wickliffe Kast

If you believe, you will receive
whatever you ask for in prayer.

MATTHEW 21:22

Cpl. Phillip W. Coon, Regular Army, Serial No.18052580
31st Inf. Regiment, 2nd BN - "H" Co. 4th squad - Bataan, Philippines

Phillip W. Coon was a proud member of the Muscogee (Creek) Nation

For special discounts on bulk purchases, please email
Sales@KastPublishing.com.

ISBN:978-0-9962097-2-4
Cover and book design: k lowe creative
Back cover map: www.mapsbymikereagan.com
Printed in the United States of America

A Soldier's Silent Prayer

Sherry Wickliffe Kast
Kast Publishing, LLC

DEDICATION

To the memory of two of the strongest people I know –
my dad, Phillip W. Coon, and my mother,
Helen Simmer Coon. Your survival spirit and love
for the Lord inspires me daily.

I am proud to be your son. Your legacy will live
on for generations to come.

Michael Coon

To my dad and mom, Bill and Mary Lue Wickliffe,
thank you always for believing in me and encouraging me.

I am forever grateful for your love and support.

Sherry Wickliffe Kast

CONTENTS

FOREWORD

As Native people, every day that we get up to take on a new day we have to learn how to walk in two worlds with one spirit. One world asks that we continue the traditions and culture passed down through the generations. And the other world asks us to assimilate with today's society. I believe Phillip W. Coon walked in two worlds with one spirit.

Phillip came from very humble beginnings and lived his life in a way that was very successful. He was very proud of his military background, having served in the Philippines during World War II.

He was a Bataan Death March survivor and a former prisoner of war. Phillip rarely talked about what happened to him on the 62-mile Bataan Death March or his time as a POW. However, he always shared about his belief and faith, and how others back home were always praying for him.

In Indian country, the elders say we are all related. Before I was ever born I believe I had a connection with Phillip. My dad was from the Okemah area in eastern Oklahoma and Phillip was from there as well. We shared stories of relatives from that area. We had the same interests and we both liked talking to each other in our native language. He was known for being a good baseball player and I loved to play ball as well. He attended Haskell Institute in Lawrence, Kansas, and later I attended the same all-Indian school.

I previously served as a host for a local CBS television show in Tulsa, Oklahoma, and was honored to have Phillip as one of my guests. He loved talking about the military, friends that he made, and prayer. Phillip believed his survival was due to prayer, as well as his excellent physical condition. Sports always played a role in Phillip's life and he was later inducted into the Haskell Hall of Fame for lettering in baseball and basketball three years in a row.

It was a true honor to know Phillip. I was equally honored to have known his wife Helen. They were deeply involved in church work, serving alongside my aunt and uncle. Through my aunt and uncle, I was so glad to have met Phillip and Helen when I was young. As I became an elder in the tribe and got involved with tribal politics, Phillip was one of the first individuals I would go to for counsel. He was always very encouraging and in many ways treated me like one of his sons.

A national tribal treasure and outstanding member of our tribe, Phillip was a Muscogee (Creek) Nation Principal Chief Medal of Honor recipient. He and Helen are both members of the tribe's Hall of Fame. It is a privilege for me to write this foreword for Phillip W. Coon's biography. I know you will be inspired by his survival story, his faith in God, and service to our country. He was no doubt a great soldier among "The Greatest Generation."

George Tiger, Principal Chief
Muscogee (Creek) Nation

ACKNOWLEDGMENTS

This book would not have been possible without Michael Coon's vision and passion to share the incredible story of survival and faith of his father, Phillip W. Coon.

A special thank you is extended to Muscogee (Creek) Nation Principal Chief George Tiger and the Muscogee (Creek) Nation National Council for their support and generosity in making this project possible.

The Muscogee Nation Communications Department played a critical role in providing access to numerous newspaper articles and photos of Mr. Coon. Thank you, Christina Good Voice and Sterling J. Cosper for your assistance.

Numerous individuals were interviewed regarding Mr. Coon's influence on their lives. These individuals included Muscogee (Creek) Nation Chief George Tiger, Edna Pickering, Gerald Wofford, Kenneth Taryole, Robert Coffey, Daniel Wind III, David Foster, Janet Mathews, Moe Moyer, John and Fran Harrison, John Mims, Doris Ingersoll, and Kat McLaughlin. Thank you for your time and kind words.

Additionally, this book would not have happened without the assistance from numerous organizations, including the Sapulpa Historical Museum Society, Inc. and The Euchee Indian School Alumni Association, Rutgers University Oral History Archives, Battling Bastards of Bataan, The Lawton Constitution, The Ride Home, National Archives, and the National Prisoner of War Museum and National Park Service in Andersonville, Georgia.

8

And finally, thank you Michael Coon, Sherry Kast, Gerald Wofford, and Debbie Mason for your outstanding research; Heather D. Koontz for your editing skills, Federico Baldassarre and his knowledge of the Battle of Bataan, Linda Sargent for proofing, and Teresa Eash for her support and encouragement during this process. And to Yukako Ibuki, your assistance in providing information and photos regarding the Japanese/American POW Friendship Program is greatly appreciated.

Three generations of the Coon Family proudly served and continue to serve God and country.
Top photo: From left, Michael, Phillip, and Michael Keith.
Bottom photo: From left, Michael Keith, Phillip, and Michael.

VETERAN'S DAY SPEECH

We Will Not Forget – Veterans Who Gave Their Lives
November 11, 1990

"Veteran's Day" – A time to honor our war dead who believed in our country, our freedom, and our way of life enough to fight bravely and even die for all we, as a nation, hold dear.

With heartfelt emotion we gratefully thank our war dead. They cannot hear us thank them for giving their lives in order that we might remain free. They cannot hear us praise their mighty deeds in battle on foreign soil. They cannot see the floral wreaths presented in their honor. They cannot see the tears shed by loved ones left behind. They cannot see each of us stand a little taller as our flag is raised and waves in the breeze. They cannot feel the pride swell within us as we sing "The Star Spangled Banner."

But they knew in life – because they experienced it themselves – that AMERICA, and all she stands for to each AMERICAN, is worth defending, worth fighting for, worth dying for.

They, our war dead who gave their very lives, are not truly dead. They survive as long as we take their torch of freedom, hold it high, bear it with dignity and honor, and pursue to a triumphant finish the race of freedom and peace for all peoples everywhere.

Phillip W. Coon

CHAPTER 1
STRENGTH TO SURVIVE

Guided by moonlight, Phillip Coon was running for his life. He had to get out of the jungle. The young Army foot soldier was on the front lines in the Philippines fighting against Japan's 14th Imperial Army. He was among 12,000 American and 78,000 Filipino troops defending the Bataan Peninsula in the Pacific Theater during World War II.

For what seemed like two days, Phillip tried to get out of the python- and malaria- infested jungle. He was trying to get to the Mariveles mountains at the southernmost tip of Bataan. If he could get there, he could then get to the island of Corregidor two miles away, across the channel from Cabcaben, in the Bay of Manila. At Corregidor, Phillip believed he would be safe and fed along with the U.S. forces who were still fighting the Japanese.

Phillip was born a full-blood Muscogee (Creek) Indian. As a young Indian boy growing up in eastern Oklahoma in the 1920s, he didn't have the easiest of childhoods. Phillip's father was an alcoholic. One night his drunken father fired a shot at whom he thought was an intruder breaking through the gate on the fence that surrounded the family's house. Phillip's dad had mistakenly shot and killed his wife's father, Phillip's grandfather.

Phillip's mother would succumb to sickness before his teenage years. No one knew what ailed her and she eventually passed away. The young boy from Oklahoma would suffer additional losses and with no one to care for him, he would be sent away to an Indian boarding school for orphans where he was subjected to a disciplined and regimented lifestyle. Ironically, the boarding school lifestyle would be of great benefit to Phillip as a soldier in the Army.

At age 21, Phillip had already endured a lifetime of struggles. And while the young recruit was trying to get to Mariveles for refuge, he would have to rely on his survival skills, athletic ability, and independent spirit like never before. He would also draw strength from his older sister Sophie, whom he loved dearly. He would have to grasp the traditions and culture of the Muscogee people that had been handed down to him through the generations.

"I didn't make it," Phillip said about trying to get to Mariveles.

"I was caught on the trail with about 75 other soldiers heading for the mountains."

"I was captured."

Tired, worn out, hungry and thirsty, Phillip had become a prisoner of the Japanese Imperial Army.

He was forced to assemble with the other soldiers in Mariveles. There he was put in a column of men, four wide, and then forced to march north along Bataan's East Road. Years later, this march came to be known as the Bataan Death March – one of the most heinous atrocities of World War II. It would also mark the beginning of three-and-a-half years of hard labor, imprisonment and cruelty for Phillip, as well as thousands of American soldiers.

Phillip could have cracked anytime during this tumultuous period of his life, but didn't. He would find solace on this nightmarish journey with the help of four comrades. The bond of brotherhood Phillip developed with three Native American buddies from southern states and one friend from Indiana, as well as the bond Phillip would experience with the Lord gave him strength to survive the brutal torture and countless acts of humiliation he was about to endure.

CHAPTER 2
GROWING UP ON INDIAN LANDS

Phillip William Coon was born May 28, 1919 to Taylor and Missaley Johnson Coon and raised in the small rural Oklahoma community of Mason, located about 15 miles north of Okemah in Okfuskee County. A full-blooded Indian, Phillip was born into the Muscogee (Creek) Nation, one of the largest tribes encompassing 11 counties in eastern Oklahoma. The Muscogee people are a strong people who have a long, rich history steeped in tradition.[1]

Early ancestors of the Muscogee constructed earthen pyramids along the rivers that spanned the Southeastern United States as part of elaborate towns and ceremonial complexes. In the early 19th century, the United States Indian policy focused on the removal of the Muscogee and the other Southeastern tribes west to areas beyond the Mississippi River in what is commonly known as the Trail of Tears.[2]

Today, the Muscogee people continue gathering at their ceremonial grounds, a place where they can relate back to their ancestors and traditions. With 16 ceremonial grounds, they gather to celebrate the Creator and life with traditional songs and dances.

Phillip was born into the Alligator Clan of the Nuyaka tribal town, located near Mason. As a youngster, Phillip would join other boys to prepare the ceremonial grounds at Nuyaka for three-day spiritual gatherings. He would help clean the grounds, fix a fence, and haul water, among other responsibilities. The young men fasted during the three days and then enjoyed a feast, along with community members, on Sunday. The time spent at Nuyaka would shape Phillip's life and define his character.[3]

While growing up in Okfuskee County, Phillip helped out on the family farm. Families who lived in the county raised cattle, and grew cotton and other crops. Phillip's family was no different. Although the family didn't have much, Phillip would be the first to say they had everything they needed on the farm.

"Our family lived on Indian lands. It was in a rural area. The land was good. We were poor, but we had electricity," Phillip said.

"My dad plowed the field by a walker. You might say he did farm labor to support our family. We had a garden, big garden. He knew how to sow seeds and he raised a crop. My father knew how to grow fruit. We had grapes and two kinds of peaches – Elberta and yellow. We also grew peanuts."[4]

Being a country boy from Oklahoma meant that Phillip was outdoors more often than not. And like most boys, Phillip would play outside all day if he could. He didn't much care for riding horses so he walked everywhere. Phillip would walk to town. He'd walk along the family farm. Later, when Phillip went to a boarding school, he would sometimes walk 22 miles from Sapulpa to Bristow to catch a bus for Okemah to go home. He'd reverse the trip on the way back to school.

Phillip was good at building things with his hands. One afternoon, he took great care to make a swing for the big oak tree that stood tall in their back yard, sanding all four sides of the seat to complete the perfect swing. He was also a natural athlete and he loved to play baseball. He couldn't wait for summertime when he religiously took to the diamond every week.

At a young age, Phillip learned to be neighborly. He would often draw a bucket of water and take it to the men working out in the field so they could have a cool drink of water.

"That was good times for our family," Phillip said of his childhood.[5]

That was until sickness and death came into the Coon family.

Phillip was one of Taylor and Missaley's five children. He had an older sister named Sophie and three younger siblings – Issac, Chester and Estella. His brothers and younger sister died in the mid-1920s and then his mom, Missaley, died in December 1927. As a young boy, Phillip couldn't recall the details of his mother's death, but remembered how people would come to the house to help out.

"Things were pretty rough and I didn't know what kind of sickness she had," Phillip said. "But in a rural area when a person died, some families would bring a covered dish or come help clean house or help look out after children. Just being good neighbors, you might say."

Following Missaley's death, Taylor found himself unable to care for and raise his son and daughter so he sent them away to live with their grandma.

"She was a good cook, my grandma. I liked potatoes and she would bake some sweet potatoes for me. We had crawfish. And stew," Phillip said.

"Grandma always made me wash my hands. She would also tell me to go get some wood and I chopped wood for the cook stove every day."

"We had a garden. My job was to keep the little pigs off the vegetable garden," Phillip said. "We had fruit. There were a lot of blackberries, a lot of mulberries."

And when the apples were ripe, Phillip would pick them and eat them until he'd get sick.

"I sure liked my grandma," said Phillip, who enjoyed going with her to the grocery store in nearby Mason or Kellyville. They would go to town by horse and buggy, and there was a box seat in the back for Phillip. "The horse's tail would go straight up and I'd say, 'cen takebv,' which is Creek for 'Are you ready?'" Phillip said. "Off we'd go to town."

Phillip was grateful for the time he spent with his grandmother. However, that time was short-lived as his grandmother died within a year of Phillip and Sophie moving in with her.

"When grandma passed away, she went to bed and she never woke up," Phillip said. "She was gone."

It was at this time Phillip's father dropped him off at an Indian boarding school in Sapulpa, Oklahoma, where the scared youngster didn't know anyone and was prohibited him from speaking his native Creek language. Not only did he have to cope with the loss of his grandmother, he would be separated from Sophie who was sent to a girl's boarding school in Eufaula, Oklahoma.

Boarding schools were a place where many parents who were unable to care for their children would send them so they could be fed, clothed, and most importantly, receive an education. This was the case with Phillip and Sophie.

Taylor would eventually re-marry and Phillip would gain two half-brothers and a half-sister – Charley, Italy, and Edna Mae. However, he and Sophie would always be the closest of siblings despite being sent away to different schools.

1.   "Chief George Tiger's Greeting," accessed February 21, 2015, http://www.muscogeenation-nsn.gov/Homepage/chiefgreeting. html.
2.   "Muscogee (Creek) Nation History," accessed February 21, 2015, http://www.muscogeenation-nsn.gov/Pages/History/history.html.
3.   Harjo, Nelson. Interview by author. Telephone interview. Oklahoma City, Oklahoma, February 19, 2015.
4.   Coon, Phillip W. Oral History Interview, Herndon, Virginia, April 15, 2007, by Shaun Illingworth, Rutgers Oral History Archives.
5.   Coon, Phillip W. Interview by author. Personal interview. Sapulpa, Oklahoma, August 2013.

CHAPTER 3
BOARDING SCHOOL LIFE

From 1928 to 1937, Phillip attended Euchee Boarding School, an Indian mission school for orphans and other children whose families were unable to care for them.

The Euchee Boarding School was located near the bustling town of Sapulpa, Oklahoma, about 14 miles south of Tulsa. It was established in 1891 by the Presbyterian Mission Board and opened in 1894. In the beginning the school was co-educational and had only three buildings, including two dormitories and a three-room schoolhouse, all located on 40 acres of tribal property about a mile east of Sapulpa. The road to campus was lined with catalpa trees. And enormous oaks added beauty to the campus.

The Creek Council appointed a Methodist and Euchee minister, Noah Gregory, as the schools' first superintendent. Henry Land and William Sapulpa then followed as second and third superintendents.

The school was maintained by appropriations from Creek funds until 1928 when it was taken over and supported entirely by federal appropriations under supervision of the United States Indian Office. In 1947, the school was closed when the land and buildings were sold to Oklahoma School District No. 33 for use by the public schools.[1]

"I came to boarding school in about the first grade and grew up in the boarding school," Phillip said.

By the time Phillip went to Euchee, it had become a boarding school for boys only.

"There were no girls there. It was all boys when I went there," Phillip said. "I got one dress shirt and one plaid shirt. That was it."

The school, which tried to make a "white man" out of the "red man," was not for every student. The students were forced to learn English and couldn't speak their native tongue. If they did, they would often get hit by a teacher with a ruler. Some students suffered extreme homesickness and left school. Others, like Phillip, embraced the challenge, as scary as it might have been.

Students at Euchee worked in gardens and in chicken houses located on the campus, as well as the dairy barn. Once their chores were done, they had the opportunity to play sports. This was one activity that provided Phillip with a level of comfort as he thrived in sports while at boarding school.

"I remember well my Euchee Mission days. Mr. Homer Wright was the Superintendent of the school at the time. Euchee Mission School was located right on the campus that accommodated first through the fourth grades while fifth and sixth graders attended Woodlawn Middle School just off Euchee campus and was a part of the Sapulpa Public School District. The Euchee Mission seventh and eighth graders walked to Washington Junior High School which was about a one mile walk. After completion of the eighth grade, the mission boys chose one of several Bureau of Indian Affairs high schools that included Chilocco, Haskell Institute or Sequoyah. There were several more BIA high schools located in the western part of Oklahoma, however, most students whose home areas were in the eastern section of Oklahoma elected to enroll at Chilocco or Haskell. There were a few who chose Sequoyah High School. I chose to go to Haskell after my ninth grade in 1937.

I had many friends at Euchee but I remember some of my best friends that included Joe Grayson, Elmer Harjo, Jacob Jimboy, Sam Brown and Alexander Hardridge. I played baseball and basketball while I was at Euchee and I remember Johnson Fields who played center on the basketball team. He usually would hang around our goal during a game and us little fast guys would rush the ball down to him and he would score. Most of our games, even championship games, we played that way. Lloyd Williams was another player I remember. We would play other Indian schools that included Pawnee Indian School, Concho Indian School and Riverside Indian School located in Anadarko, Oklahoma. I lettered in basketball and baseball and I still have those letters among my keepsakes.

I remember boys who were in school the same time I was. I remember Homer Lee Curtis and his brothers Carl, Jim Roe, and Leonard."

Phillip Coon
Euchee Indian School Alumni Voices

Euchee Mission was not the right path for all who entered. Some students suffered extreme homesickness and departed on their own. Others appreciated the opportunity to learn. While the curriculum might have included milking cows, making gardens, washing clothes and other chores that taught them how to meet life head-on, it also embraced subjects that would carry the students through high school and on to more sophisticated learning.[2]

During the summer after Phillip finished school at Euchee, he played summer ball. Phillip's love for baseball helped him secure a spot on the 1937 Okemah American Legion baseball team as a center fielder. Coached by city attorney and former University of Oklahoma baseball player Dick Jones, the team became the Oklahoma state champions and then made the national playoffs. They beat teams from Oklahoma, Nebraska, and Texas.

As a reward for doing so well, the team was awarded with a trip to New York to watch the Yankees play the St. Louis Cardinals. St. Louis was Phillip's favorite team and his favorite player was Cardinals pitcher Dizzy Dean. Upon hearing of this trip of a lifetime, Phillip had already started high school at Haskell Institute in Lawrence, Kansas (now Haskell Indian Nations University). He hitchhiked from Kansas to Oklahoma for his dad to sign a permission slip because he was still a minor at age 17. His dad refused to sign the permission slip, telling Phillip that he needed to stay in school.

Phillip never forgave his dad, but that didn't keep him from playing the game he loved. He continued to play baseball, making the team at Haskell Institute and lettering in the sport three years in a row – 1939, 1940, and 1941. He lettered in basketball all three years as well.

1.   Tommy Cummings, "About Euchee Mission," *Muscogee Nation News*, June 1990, 4.
2.   Gene Leitka and Associates. *Euchee Indian School Alumni Voices*. Albuquerque, New Mexico: The Euchee Indian School Alumni Association. Transcriptions Recorded by Jim Hubbard, Sapulpa Historical Museum Society, Inc., 2000.

CHAPTER 4
HASKELL INSTITUTE

Like most of the mission boys who attended Euchee Boarding School, Phillip went to high school in Lawrence, Kansas, to study a commercial trade at Haskell Institute. The boys from Oklahoma were joined by other Indian students from all across the country, but mainly from the states of Montana, Arizona, and New Mexico. One of those students from Oklahoma was Alex Mathews, who was a member of the Pawnee Nation. Alex would not only become a classmate of Phillip's, but he would be a fellow comrade in the Philippines and a lifelong friend.

Haskell was a government school and the campus housed boys and girls dormitories. Upon arrival on campus, the students were issued two pairs of shoes – one pair of work shoes and one pair of dress shoes that they called stogies.

Phillip went to Haskell to become a painter and he also studied shoe repair. He could be spotted on campus with paint all over his white hat, white shirt, and white shoes. When Phillip wasn't in his painter's clothes, he always dressed very nice, wearing a white shirt with dark trousers. He was not one to wear a tie.

It was also at Haskell that Phillip began to date Helen Simmer. Helen was also full-blood Creek. Phillip actually met Helen years earlier in Oklahoma at Fish Pound, her ceremonial ground in Cromwell. Phillip was about 5' 5" tall and Helen stood chin-high next to him. Helen was pretty and with her beautiful olive skin she didn't have much of a need to wear makeup. Phillip and Helen seemed to be a perfect couple. He was so personable. She was friendly and had a mellow demeanor. The couple was often spotted walking hand-in-hand on campus or having lunch together on Saturday afternoons.

The students at Haskell would have a get together on Saturday nights at the campus gymnasium and dance to the music of Glenn Miller and Harry James. Helen and Phillip would jitterbug the night away.

On Sunday mornings, Phillip joined Helen and nearly 20 students as they always went downtown to the First Baptist Church of Lawrence, Kansas. It was springtime during one of his years at Haskell that Brother Thomas baptized Phillip and that's when he dedicated his life to the Lord.[1]

---

1.   Pickering, Edna. Interview by author. Tape recording. Norman, Oklahoma, August 2014.

Haskell Institute: Phillip Coon and Helen Simmer (left) with friends.

CHAPTER 5
SEND ME TO THE PHILIPPINES

Phillip graduated in 1941 from Haskell Institute and stayed in Lawrence, Kansas.

"The year I graduated, General Hershey (director of the Selective Service System) made a nationwide speech on the radio. He said the draft board is coming into effect and when you turn 21, you have to register. You go to the county seat for the draft board and put your name on the list."[1]

At the time Phillip volunteered for the military, the peace-time draft was imposed on men ages 21 to 36. In November 1942, the draft was expanded to include ages 18 to 37.[2]

Indian people were volunteering for military service at a greater percentage than any other race. Phillip was among them. He went to Douglas County, Kansas, and volunteered for foreign duty with the Army. He chose the Infantry over the Calvary because he didn't much care for riding horses.

Phillip enlisted in the U.S. Army on September 29, 1941.

"Whether they take you or not, that would be up to the medical officer when they check you out," Phillip said. "Some didn't make it who volunteered. Some were turned down. Some had a weak heart and a lot of problems. That's understandable."

"If I waited to get drafted I wouldn't have an option of where I wanted to be," Phillip said. "That's why I volunteered."

Phillip returned to Oklahoma to see his family prior to shipping out for foreign duty.

After seeing his family, Phillip's uncle Frank put him on a bus to Oklahoma City, giving him some pocket money for his trip. While in Oklahoma City, Phillip took his oath for military service before heading west to Fort McDowell, California, and eventually the Philippines.

"I volunteered for Hawaii and then I changed my mind before I signed the document for military service," Phillip said. "I had a chance to go to Panama, Puerto Rico, Alaska, Hawaii, or the Philippines."

"In Oklahoma City, they asked 'Are you sure this is where you want to go?' That's when I changed my mind."

"Send me to Philippines," Phillip told the draft board.

In the fifth grade, Phillip studied geography and he was fascinated with the Philippines. He dreamed about the eastern lands, wanting to learn more about its culture and its people.[3]

"I studied the history of people of different countries," Phillip said. "I read a little about those people over there."

Ironically, the country that inspired his youthful curiosity is also the same place that would rob his youth.[4]

1. Illingworth.
2. "This Day in History'" accessed December 14, 2014," http://www.history.com/this-day-in-history/draft-age-is-lowered-to-18.
3. Stephanie Berryhill, "Veterans tribute, World War II prisoner recalls his sacrifice for freedom," *Muscogee Nation News*, November 1991.
4. Kathryn Bell, "Creek Soldier Survivor of 'Death March,'" *Muscogee Nation News*, November 1983.

CHAPTER 6
BOARDING SCHOOL PAYS OFF

A young private in the Army, Phillip was full of dreams for the future and ready to fight for noble ideas of freedom, honor, and love for his country. When he volunteered for duty in the Philippines, he was unaware at that time, as most were, of the three-and-a-half-year nightmare he was about to experience.[1]

But before heading to the Philippines, he needed to go through Fort McDowell, a processing center for all outgoing and returning U.S. service personnel. "I got all my clothing there," Phillip said. "When you are going to the tropics you don't need wools so I got all khakis." The Army refers to its tropical clothing as khakis.

"I arrived at Fort McDowell, California, on a train at 2 a.m. in the morning," Phillip said. "Later that first morning, I heard someone hollering, 'Everybody fall out!'"

Phillip immediately responded. He was used to getting up early from when he attended boarding school.

"Come on. Get outside. Get in columns of two," the unknown voice demanded.

"I knew what they meant so I just stood there," Phillip said.

Drills followed and the Oklahoma recruit knew exactly how to follow the commands.

"He said right face. I made a right face," Phillip said. "The other boys didn't know what he meant. They just looked at him."

Sergeant said, "Just do like Coon is doing."

"Sergeant told everyone to go on up the hill and eat breakfast after drills," Phillip said. "He told me to stay put, asking if I went to military school."

"No," Phillip told the sergeant. "I went to an orphan boarding school and we used to do drills and exercise before breakfast, and I know those short commands."

Phillip recalled how his childhood days at the Euchee Boarding School would help him in the military. Not only did he do his chores while at school, Phillip, as well as the other students, also learned basic military commands.[2]

"We had to be up at six o'clock each morning, get dressed, go downstairs, and line up in formations. The school officials would hold inspections to see if our bed was properly made and our rooms were clean. They would give out commands just like the military. That's how I learned to take orders," Phillip said.

The sergeant told Phillip, "Young man, it's to your advantage that you know all those. So you are going to be all right."

Phillip always remembered how the sergeant was impressed by his knowledge of commands and appreciation for following rules. The regimented lifestyle Phillip was exposed to at boarding school would no doubt pay off for him during his military career.

"I knew the cadence and everything before I went into the military. Right rear... About face... I knew the short order commands. I knew all the basic marches. Right to black means you are marching straight ahead and turn right at a 45 degree angle. If they say left, you turn left. Left to black means you go left 45 degrees. Halt means stop right there. You can't be facing this way or that way. You have to stop. We did that every morning before breakfast. We did calisthenics and we marched in columns of two," Phillip said.

"I'm grateful for learning basic military commands and drills. I had the advantage from school. I didn't think I'd have the ambition to be a buck sergeant, but I had the advantage because I knew the basics."[3]

1. Bell.
2. Gerald Wofford, "A Native American Patriot: Phillip Coon," *Muscogee Nation News.*
3. Illingworth.

Formation line at Euchee Boarding School in the early 1900s. Learning basic military commands at school would serve Phillip well as a soldier.

Photo courtesy: Sapulpa Historical Society

CHAPTER 7
A FRIEND FOR LIFE

From Fort McDowell, Phillip was ferried on a tugboat to Fort Mason. At Fort Mason dock, Phillip would meet a buddy and friend for life.

During World War II, Fort Mason was the headquarters of the San Francisco Port of Embarkation, controlling a network of shipping facilities that spread across the Bay Area, and ultimately transporting troops and cargo to the Pacific Theater.[1]

"A small craft would take us from Fort McDowell to the main dock at Fort Mason. We'd have roll call at Fort Mason before boarding the ship. They call your name and you answer, 'First Name and Middle Initial.' When my name was called, 'Coon,' I had to say 'Phillip W.' And, when the sergeant asked me what that 'W' was for, I said, 'William.'"

At roll call, Phillip heard the name Cornsilk. Knowing Cornsilk was an Indian name, Phillip knew he would no longer be the only Indian headed to the Philippines.

Cornsilk's first name was Jacob. He stood about 6'2" and was a member of the Eastern Band of Cherokee from North Carolina. In the 19th century, the Eastern Band of Cherokee remained in the Eastern United States while other tribes moved west, or were forced to relocate.[2]

Jacob attended Chilocco Indian Agricultural School, located

in north-central Oklahoma near the Oklahoma-Kansas border. He was a gold medal boxer and a member of the Chilocco boxing team. During his senior year in 1938, Jacob left school at the beginning of the second semester to take a job as a shoe maker.[3] He later volunteered for the Army.

"Jacob stood next to me. He looked down at me," Phillip said. "He said to me, 'Hey buddy you just look like an Indian from Oklahoma.' I said, 'How do you know?' He just said, 'You look like an Indian from Oklahoma. My name is Jacob Cornsilk. I'm full-blood Cherokee. What are you?'"

"I told him my name is Phillip W. Coon. I am full-blood Creek."

"Well, put it there buddy," Jacob replied as the two shook hands. There was an instant bond between the two Indian recruits. They were headed to a faraway land and although they were from different tribes they were both comforted in knowing someone else from the same Native culture.

On October 3, 1941, Phillip, Jacob and the other recruits were immediately on their way to the Philippines aboard the USAT Willard A. Holbrook. After a brief stop in Hawaii, they were destined for Manila, known in those days as the "Pearl of the Orient."

"Jake was a big fella, a big old Cherokee," Phillip said. "I'm a little guy and he made about two of me. As we were sailing out of the San Francisco Bay, Jacob asked me to walk with him to the back of the ship. He kept saying, 'Hey buddy, would you go to the back of the ship?'"[4]

And there on the back of the ship the two Indian buddies stood watching the Golden Gate Bridge go out of sight.

"There were tears in his eyes. I looked up there out of the corner of my eye and there was a tear rolling down his cheek. He is weeping solid. I asked, 'What's up Jake?' Then he cleared his throat and asked, 'Do you see that picture, that Golden Gate Bridge? You see it? It is going to go out of sight pretty soon. We are going to pull away from that picture. I want you to stand right here until that picture goes out of sight. When we come back, if we come back, we'll come to the front of the ship and stand right here. That picture will come back to us. We will come back to it. That's the first thing you see when you come back to the shoreline. That's the first thing you see – The Golden Gate Bridge. Then, we'll know we are home.'"

Jacob made Phillip promise that they would go to the front of the ship and watch as the bridge came back into focus upon their return to America.

"He made me shake on that promise and although it didn't mean much to me at the time, I knew it meant a lot to him," Phillip said. "So we stood there and watched until the bridge disappeared on the horizon."[5]

1. "Fort Mason History," accessed September 2014, http://www.nps.gov/goga/historyculture/fort-mason-page-2.htm.
2. "Eastern Band of Cherokee," accessed February 21, 2015, http://nc-cherokee.com.
3. The 1938 Chiloccoan Senior Class Annual. Chilocco, Oklahoma: Senior Class of 1938 at the Chilocco Indian Agricultural School, 9.
4. Illingworth.
5. Bell.

CHAPTER 8
TRAINED TO JUNGLE FIGHT

Phillip was one of six soldiers from his tribe to serve in the Philippines; five would defend Corregidor and Phillip would be the only Creek to fight on Bataan. These soldiers were from little farms near such places as Preston or Twin Hills in Oklahoma, to bigger places like Eufaula or Tulsa. Some were raised in the Muscogee (Creek) churches, others were raised in the traditional ceremonial tribal towns. Either way, they were to be involved with the largest world event of the 20th century.[1]

Phillip arrived at Manila's Pier 7, in the Philippines on October 23, 1941. He and the other recruits were put on trucks and sent to Fort McKinley, south of the city of Manila, where they underwent rigorous basic training. They lived in what was called tent city as they waited for their barracks to be repainted.

"We lived in tents. We had our foot lockers in there for our personal things. We would be out in the field doing exercises in the morning because the heat was terrible in the afternoon," Phillip said. "We always kept to our routine in the morning. We'd come in at 10 and we were off the rest of the day. We'd do a little book study under the shade tree."

The recruits trained early in the morning to avoid the extremely high afternoon temperatures. And although Phillip spent years playing outside under the sweltering Oklahoma sun, he wasn't prepared for the tropical heat he would experience in the Philippines.

"Oklahoma is hot, but boy tropical heat is worse. The tropical heat is tremendous. Tremendous! Humidity is high. I sweated all the time. Maybe that's why I didn't put weight on. There is nowhere in the USA like the Philippines. The Louisiana swamp, they say is pretty close, but I've seen that and it doesn't compare to the Philippines."

The raw recruits not only had to get used to the tropical heat, they would have to survive the python-infested jungles, learn how to maneuver around the rough terrain, and crawl through elephant grass.

"The jungle is a lot different than Europe where it was wide open terrain and you could see where someone was shooting from," Phillip said. "Everything was different, so they taught us to jungle fight."

"We wore canvas leggings with the lace on the side and buckles up to the knees because we were in the jungles. We had a course laid out. We'd get on our stomach and crawl like a snake, crawling through elephant grass that could grow up to 10 feet tall. That's how we trained over there."

There were so many things in the Philippines that Phillip never imagined he would see or experience.

"I used to watch Tarzan pictures when I was a kid. And I'd see him swing on those vines," Phillip said. "I never thought I'd see something like that. A grove of those vines are just like thick and wide worms. There were a lot of vines, just popping up in the rough terrain."

And although Phillip had seen pythons at the zoo back home, he never expected to see anything like those he would encounter in the jungle. Even more surprising to Phillip was when he learned that those pythons would supplement his food rations. After the second month of fighting and enduring extreme food shortages, the men on Bataan would joke, "If it moves, it's food."

"I know creation has a lot of different things," Phillip said. "I never expected to see anything like that – those pythons. They say they would get big. They sleep all day and roam at night. They get out at night and hunt something to eat. They swallow them wild boars. They said they would swallow humans. They swallow a lot of those Aetas (indigenous people) – little people like me. I'm short, but they are little people."

Although puzzled by the creation of pythons, Phillip knew God had made a lot of things that he could use in life for guidance. Such was the case with moonlight as Phillip depended on the brightness of the moon to help guide him through the jungle.

"Sergeant said we had a lot of guys that would wander off and forget which way they came. If you make a wrong turn in the nighttime, you'd get lost. You wouldn't know where you are at; not until the moon is out. Then you could get your bearing," Phillip said. "The moonlight was real pretty. I could tell time by the moon especially when I was on guard through the night. I could look up and say it was about 2 o'clock." [2]

1. Gerald Wofford, "Creek Veterans saw war differently," *Muscogee Nation News*, November 2003.
2. Illingworth.

CHAPTER 9
31ST INFANTRY REGIMENT –
THE POLAR BEARS

After completing basic training, the recruits returned to Manila. They were stationed in the "Intramuros" section of Manila, the oldest, historic district known to the Americans as the "Walled City."

"It's something to see," Phillip said, referring to the Walled City. "The Spanish built it, so they would be safe from invaders within its fortress walls, surrounded by a moat. You can't scale that wall."

Phillip and the other soldiers were billeted at Estado de Mayor, located in southeast Manila and overlooking Manila Bay and the Pasig River.

The soldiers were assigned to various companies and battalions. Phillip, a foot soldier, was assigned to the 31st Infantry Regiment as a .30 caliber machine gunner (M1919 Browning), a position for which he had an uncanny prowess and skill. He was assigned to machine gun company H. His buddy Jacob wanted to be assigned to the same squad as Phillip but was assigned to rifle company G. Both companies G and H were part of the 2nd Battalion.

The 31st Infantry Regiment is unique in that it was the only regular Army unit to have its entire service on foreign land. The 31st Infantry Regiment was formed at Fort William

McKinley, Philippine Islands on August 13, 1916. In the spring of 1918, the 31st moved from Manila's tropics to the bitter cold of Siberia. Its mission, left vague by a deeply divided administration, was to prevent allied war material left sitting on the docks at Vladivostok from being looted during the Russian Revolution.

For the next two years, the 31st and its sister regiment, the 27th Infantry, fought off bands of Manchurian and Cossack bandits and Red revolutionaries trying to gain control of the Trans-Siberian Railroad and the Suchan Mines. They also dissuaded their 40,000 Japanese "allies" from making claims on Russian territory. When the smoke cleared, 16 members of the 31st had earned the Distinguished Service Cross in a two-year war few Americans even knew was being fought.

For its service in Siberia, the 31st Infantry became known as "the Polar Bear regiment," adopting a silver Polar Bear as its insignia, which was designed in Manila by one of the country's best silversmiths, Crispulo Zamora.

Returning to the Philippines in 1920, the 31st garrisoned the old Walled City of Manila until February 1932 when Japanese troops invaded the Chinese city of Shanghai. Reinforcing the 4th Marines and a predominately British International Force, the 31st Infantry protected Shanghai's International Settlement (The Concessions) from incursions by either side. The 31st Infantry returned to Manila in July 1932.

Soldiers of the 31st infantry proudly uphold their motto *Omnia Pro Patria* (All for country).[1]

Phillip had become a Polar Bear.

Phillip was never around guns at home when he was a kid. His dad always told him to leave guns alone, especially his gun that was kept by the front door. Although it was never loaded, Phillip remembers his father's stern directive regarding his personal gun, "This don't belong to you. Don't you mess with this. Don't even look at it. You have no business touching it."

And although Phillip never shot a gun, much less picked one up, he heeded his uncle's advice prior to leaving for the Philippines. "When you become a soldier, you are going to carry a gun," his uncle said. "When you shoot, I want you to make that first shot count. If you miss whoever you are shooting at, he's going to shoot at you."[2]

"I just finished up the training and ended up with the 2nd Battalion machine gun company. We had .30s and .50s machine guns, and trench warmers – those are hand grenades, shaped like pineapples. I learned how to throw grenades," Phillip said.

"To my surprise, I was a gunner. I didn't feel discriminated against (in the Army). I took care of my own basic and I learned all I could. I was 2nd squad, 4th section. The gunners carried a .45 pistol and hand grenades all the time," Phillip said. "I never messed with guns growing up and I didn't know I was going to wind up that way."

"I finally qualified for .30 caliber. I found it just fascinating."

1.   31st Infantry Regiment, "The Polar Bears," A Brief History, 1916-1997.
2.   "World War II A Muscogee (Creek) Retrospect," Muscogee Nation Communications Department, 1996.

CHAPTER 10
JAPANESE ATTACK ON PEARL HARBOR AND THE PHILIPPINES

When Phillip made his choice to go to the Philippines, he didn't realize the United States would be on the verge of conflict. However, Phillip, as well as the rest of the Armed Forces of the United States, closely watched the Imperial Government of Japan. They knew that hostilities existed between the two countries.

Phillip had just finished his basic training toward the end of November 1941 and two weeks later, the Japanese attacked Pearl Harbor on Sunday, December 7, 1941. The American Pacific Naval Fleet suffered heavy losses in lives and ships. The Fleet was incapacitated and could not, in that state, defend American interest in the Pacific Rim and in Asia.[1] In the aftermath of Pearl Harbor, America declared war on Japan and Germany.

As the U.S. was plunged into World War II, Phillip's commanding sergeant prepared his soldiers.

"It was on a Monday. We were doing our rehearsing. We were training to keep us intact, keep us in tune. We were out in the field and we heard that bugle call," Phillip said.

"The sergeant of my platoon said, 'Everybody get your gear ready and trot back to the tent.' They call it double time, you trot and half run, so we double timed in."

"Upon arriving back at camp, our commander was standing there on top of the jeep with his arms folded. He kept hollering, 'Hurry up! Hurry up!' The staff sergeant, using his bull horn, yelled for everyone to be quiet and then gave the bull horn to our commander."

"Listen to this. Here it is. Pearl Harbor has been bombed!" The commander repeated this three times. "We are at war! Get your gear! Get all your ammunition! Get your field packs! We are going to load up the vehicles and we have to get to Subic Bay, northwest of the Bataan Peninsula. We are expecting the paratroopers to land and our duty is to stop them! Those who just joined the company, this is where you show your stuff. This is going to be the Real McCoy."[2]

"That was a job moving our equipment," Phillip said. "We were short of trucks. We were short of vehicles. We didn't have enough vehicles. We had some little jeeps. They gave us city buses, old city buses. The diesel mechanics got them running and we took a lot of little bushes, splattering and coloring them green."

Eight hours later, across the International Date Line, on December 8, the Japanese made the first of many attacks that would lead to the takeover of Bataan and Corregidor, Philippines. The 31st Infantry Regiment headed for the Bataan Peninsula to intercept Japanese paratroopers.

The Japanese didn't drop any paratroopers. They stormed ashore in the Lingayen Gulf, north of Bataan and far south in Lamon Bay. The United States Army Forces in the Far

East (USAFFE) were divided into the Northern Luzon Force, under the command of General Wainwright, and the Southern Luzon Force, under the command of General Parker.

Japanese planes attacked U.S. military installations all over the Philippines and a 31st Infantry sergeant became the campaign's first fatality when Camp John Hay was bombed.

Nichols Field and Clark Field lost almost all their bombers in a sneak attack while the planes were on the ground. There was some confusion as to whether the planes should attack the Japanese air bases on Formosa, escape to the safety of the far off Del Monte Air Base in Mindanao, or stay on their tarmacs in Luzon. Their inactions proved their doom. Most were destroyed as they sat on their tarmacs at the various air bases.

General Douglas MacArthur, Commander of the Filipino-American Forces, decided to meet the Japanese at their points of landing. This course of action deviated from the original War Plan Orange, devised prior to World War II, which called for the American forces to withdraw into the Bataan Peninsula in case of attack.[3]

When the Japanese landed on the islands in Luzon, the 26th Cavalry Regiment, Philippine Army Divisions, and the U.S. Tank Battalions were waiting. The 26th Cavalry and its horses would suffer greatly. General Masaharu Homma and his 43,000-man 14th Imperial Army – a mixture of Japan's elite soldiers and many of their inexperienced units – quickly converged upon the predominantly poorly trained American garrison forces and the poorly trained, in some cases untrained, Filipino soldiers.[4] Another 12,000 Japanese soldiers landed in the southern islands of Mindanao.

The U.S. soldiers had two strikes against them when the war broke out. They were green and relatively untrained; especially their comrades, the Filipinos, and many were issued World War I equipment.

"We weren't ready for war. We were not ready," Phillip said. "We just didn't have modern equipment."

"We used World War I leftover ammunition and helmets. The ammunitions had been stored too long. About a third of our ammo were duds. Our clips wouldn't go off. That was discouraging. We had .45 pistols with five shells per clip and only four would fire. They issued .50 caliber and .30 caliber machine guns. I was a machine gunner and I had to fight with an old World War I water-cooled machine gun. Even our helmets were World War I. We called them wash pan helmets. Just round, they barely covered up your ears. When I came back (home), I was surprised to see the new helmets the Army issued."

"They issued hand grenades. We called them pineapples. They were shaped like little pineapples but they were steel. I had two of them on my belt, but I got rid of them 'cause when you lie down and rest you might turn over and pull that pin out and blow yourself up. I told my corporal, 'Somebody might reach over there and say, 'What's that?' and pull that pin and blow both of us up.'"

"If we had modern equipment, I think we'd been all right," Phillip said. "Our problem was we ran out of ammunition. We didn't have any supplies coming in."[5]

The men on Bataan were besieged with no available Navy to break the Japanese blockade which tightened their grip around them. Also, in those days, distances proved to be overwhelming, even with the best Navy or Air Force. The Philippines was simply too far away, taking several weeks to get there by ship. One had to have advanced bases in those Pacific Islands to be able to supply such a distant post as the Philippines. After the quick demise of American bases in the Pacific, as well as the damage done to the fleet in Hawaii, it became impossible to resupply the men on Bataan. It had to be done by retaking the various islands in the Pacific and re-establishing supply lines, one island at a time. This took at least two years, so the men on Bataan received no help in their far off post.[6]

"Our medical supplies, ammo and food rations were low," Phillip said. "First we killed the horses used by the 26th Cavalry and then we had to kill water buffalo to eat, and even they ran out. We killed those crabs and had to eat them all up."

Inadequate food and water rations, malaria, beriberi, and other diseases with no medical supplies left the troops in a devastated condition.

"But we were young and trained as soldiers and we just gave it all we had," Phillip said.

Phillip recalled some of his first heat of battle with the Japanese, at Layak Junction, in northern most Bataan. They were to fight to keep the Culo Bridge open, so it could be used by the other retreating USAFFE units and protect the entrance onto Bataan's East Road.

Phillip's leader was an expert marksman and would handle the .30 caliber machine gun if an enemy attack was imminent. As Phillip tells it, the military standard is that the corporal, or second in command, would take over the gunner duties if an enemy bullet injured or took the life of the sergeant. But Phillip's leader did not have full trust of his second in command so he told Phillip, "If anything happens to me, I want you to take over."[7]

"The Japanese field artillery laid a heavy barrage on us for six hours without letting up," Phillip said. "This was my first under-fire experience and I saw mango trees as big as oak trees here in Oklahoma split under the mortar bombings."

"Have you ever seen a coconut tree with big palms that goes way out? They (Japanese) are small like me. They would climb up in a tree and they stay up there. And that's how they observed what's going on and relay it. They would sneak up on you in the nighttime. We wondered how come they knew where we were. And, they were able to send communication to their headquarters and then they sent the dive bombers on us. Some of the dive bombers would hit pretty close to us. They seem to know where we were but just couldn't hit the right spot."

The Japanese also had "Photo Joe," two reconnaissance planes which hovered above sending messages back to their artillery as to their exact positions. They flew just above the range of their anti-aircraft fire, so they were undisturbed. The Americans and Filipinos could do nothing about these reconnaissance planes except take the accurate artillery fire that resulted from their presence above them.[8]

"We fought on and on in the skirmishes – growing weaker with starvation and sickness. The Japanese kept dive-bombing us and our soldiers kept losing their lives. Then our company's No. 1 machine gunner got killed there at the front line, and I had to step in and take over. It scared me to step in and take over. It scared me to think about how responsible (I would be) for the lives of the soldiers in my squad. I did the best I could."

One of the important duties of a machine gunner is to lay down fields of fire to protect the other soldiers in his unit. This was a very important job that if not done properly could result in the deaths of many of his comrades.

"I didn't ask for no war," Phillip said. "I feared for my life and I thought I might be killed at any minute."

Phillip didn't know how everyone else felt or how scared they were, but was consoled in the fact that a full-blood Indian from the Zuni Pueblo was in his squad. One of 19 Pueblos of New Mexico, the Pueblo of Zuni is located about 150 miles west of Albuquerque.

"There was this Zuni Indian, Ed Beyuka, who was the assistant gunner. He kept asking me if I was all right," Phillip said, recalling that first night of battle. "We both made it through that first attack. No matter what happened, we were with each other."

Ed was equally grateful for Phillip, especially for saving his life. During the battle, a dud would fall close to Ed at a mango grove and knock him out. Phillip and another comrade helped drag Ed to safety.

The two Indian gunners were always thankful for each other, whether it was for lifesaving heroics or for the little things such as two buddies sharing a can of sardines at midnight.[9]

"We moved around at nighttime and the moonlight was just real pretty," Phillip said. "If we stayed in one place they probably would have got all of us."

Phillip and his assistant gunner went through a lot of painful experiences together – so painful that they wouldn't talk about those experiences for about 50 years.[10]

1. "Outline of Events," accessed December 2014, Battlingbastardsbataan.com.
2. Muscogee Nation Communications Department.
3. "Outline of Events."
4. Berryhill.
5. Illingworth.
6. Baldassarre, Federico. Personal 20-year history collection on the Battle of Bataan. California, 2015.
7. Wofford.
8. Baldassarre.
9. Illingworth.
10. Beyuka, Ed. Personal letter from Ed Beyuka to Phillip Coon, Oct. 19, 1993.

CHAPTER 11
THE 31ST INFANTRY ON BATAAN

War was a different game in the Pacific. Brutality esca-
lated fast. The need for political power, compounded with
hatred for the western way of life, resulted in unimaginable
atrocities.

After the initial bombing of the Philippines, on December
8, 1941, the 31st Infantry Regiment remained in Manila
to protect the city from Japanese paratroopers which they
thought would soon be falling from the sky. They never came.
Also, their presence was needed to protect the businesses
and warehouses from potential looters.

On December 24, the 31st Infantry was ordered to leave
Manila as General MacArthur declared Manila an "Open
City" free from a military presence, hoping to spare Manila
the ravages of war. The 1st Battalion went to Corregidor,
and the 2nd and 3rd Battalions went to Subic Bay, northwest
of Bataan, to relieve the 4th Marine Regiment that was
protecting American assets at the Naval base.

A week later, on December 31, 1941, all three battalions were
ordered to go to Layak Junction, in the town of Dinalupihan,
in northern most Bataan. Their mission was to protect the East
Road going into Bataan and the Culo Bridge which was the
gateway into the peninsula. They were to hold their position

until the other units entered Bataan, especially the tanks and artillery pieces that were coming from northern and southern Luzon.

The inexperienced and poorly trained Philippine Army Divisions disintegrated almost immediately after contact with the Japanese units at these points of landing. MacArthur had to revert back to the original plan, War Plan Orange, withdrawing the Filipino-American forces into the Bataan Peninsula. By January 1942, most of the Northern and Southern Luzon forces were in place for the defense of Bataan. They were to fight for their lives stalling the Japanese advance while they waited to be resupplied and reinforced by fresh troops from the states.

The Japanese attacked their lines on January 2, 1942. The 31st Infantry held their positions for five days until January 6, when they retreated behind Bataan's first "Main Line of Resistance (MLR)," Mauban-Mabatang line. On January 9, 1942, the Japanese attacked this MLR in Mabatang on the eastern most sector of the line. On the 15th, they attacked the line in the town on Morong, in the western most sector. At this time the 31st Infantry was resting and reconstituting themselves behind this line. The 31st Infantry was now a part of II Corps in the eastern portion of the peninsula. I Corps held the western portion.

The Japanese also attacked the sector of the Mauban-Mabatang Line at a sugar plantation called Abucay Hacienda. This was held by the Philippine 51st Division. After several days of fierce fighting, members of the 51st Division, who had already been in many fights in northern Luzon, prior to entering Bataan, broke their lines and ran toward the rear. On January 16, 1942, the 31st Infantry was ordered to move forward to plug the hole and regain the ground that was lost when the 51st disintegrated. The 2nd Battalion led the counter-attack, with the 1st and 3rd Battalions following behind them. A nine-day battle ensued, in which much of the lost ground was regained and the Japanese were pushed back behind the Balantay River to their original position. The Battle of Abucay Hacienda will forever be remembered as one of the most heroic battles in U.S. military history.

While the fighting was going on in the Mauban-Mabatang Line, General MacArthur and his staff came to Bataan to view the Main Line of Resistance. MacArthur and his Chief of Staff, General Southerland, expressed their displeasure with the position of the Mauban-Mabatang Line, because they did not think that the "firing lines" favored the Bataan Defenders and they did not like the way Mt. Natib divided the line in two, separating I Corps from II Corps.

Despite their success against the Japanese, the 31st Infantry was ordered on January 25, 1942 to withdraw from the Mauban-Mabatang line and fall behind a new MLR, south of them, the Orion-Bagac Line. This withdrawal proved to be costly, because on the evening that they pulled back, the Japanese chose to counter-attack, leaving them exposed.[1]

> "Twisted and pierced by a two-week fight.
> The order comes to withdraw at night,
> And the hungry, weary, half dazed men
> Stumble South to entrench again."
> *From "Abucay Withdrawal," by Lt. Henry G. Lee*[2]

The 31st Infantry pulled back to the "Rest Area" in Cabcaben, near the field hospitals. There they ate their first warm meal in several weeks and bivouacked with the 200th Coastal Artillery from New Mexico. With the loss of so many men, whether killed, wounded, or sick, the 31st Infantry was no longer at "battle strength." Men from the 4th and 7th Chemical Warfare Aviation Units were added to their ranks to improve on this weakness. Several of their officers were transferred to other stronger units. While at the rear, they trained Philippine Army units and U.S. Air Corps units. They also ran daily patrols.

After the Battle of the Pockets and the Battle of the Points – which did not include the 31st Infantry – in the beginning of March 1942, the Japanese stopped attacking them and they entered into a quiet period they called the "Lull." This lasted for about three weeks.

It was on March 11, 1942, that General MacArthur was ordered to Australia. He left Bataan, taking only top officials with him. Although MacArthur promised to return, Phillip and his fellow soldiers felt abandoned. The Americans left on Bataan could only hope that help would come as promised. General King then became Commander of the Fil-American forces on Bataan, the Luzon Force.[3]

"I just feel like he left us holding the bag," Phillip said. "In Indian movies the chief is leading the pack. The fact that MacArthur was (giving orders) on the phone didn't gel with me."

Phillip had more admiration for the noncommissioned officers left on Bataan because they were physically there for the soldiers.[4] Phillip says he owes his life to the good judgment and advice of Section Sergeant Clyde Cole.

"I wouldn't be here today if it weren't for him. Cole kept us informed," Phillip said.

The Allied forces were able to hold the Japanese forces as long as they could.

"We turned them back several times. They had to call on extra troops to defeat us. But we didn't have anything to reach back for (to continue fighting)," Phillip said. "We kept pushing them back, but we suffered heavy casualties each time – and they just kept coming."

Unfortunately, the peninsula had not been adequately provisioned and the Navy was incapable of resupply delivery after losing much of the Pacific Fleet at Pearl Harbor. These naval vessels that would resupply the troops on Bataan were to sail from ports in the East Indies. By the second week of February that was no longer possible. The Japanese were fiercely attacking the East Indies and it would be just a matter of time before they collapsed. By the end of March, the Japanese reinforced their troops on Bataan with units from Manchuria, Malaysia, and Indo-China. They had doubled their troop strength, with an additional complimentary amount of artillery and aircraft.

Despite starvation, rampant disease, no supplies, obsolete weapons, and sometimes inoperative ammunition, the peninsula's defenders fought the Japanese – an enemy that possessed every necessity – to a standstill for four months, proving to the world that the Japanese could be stopped by a determined force, providing great insight into their fighting capabilities and propaganda value to those back home.

Although they were told that help was coming, Phillips' unit and others fought valiantly and kept the enemy at bay from January to April 1942. Although no assistance came and they felt deserted, they kept fighting.[5]

In the morning of April 3, around 10 a.m., the Fil-American troops were suddenly awakened to massive artillery fire and explosions of 1,000 and 2,000 pound bombs. The Battle of

Mount Samat had begun. The Battle of Mount Samat was also known as the Battle of the Trails.[6]

1. Baldassarre.
2. "Nothing But Praise" by Lt. Henry G. Lee, 1945.
3. "Outline of Events."
4. Berryhill.
5. Gerald Wofford, "Creek Veteran Travels to Asia to Honor Fallen," *Muscogee Nation News,* May 2014.
6. Baldassarre.

CHAPTER 12
FINAL ASSAULT ON MOUNT SAMAT

The Japanese General Masaharu Homma made his final assault in the Bataan Peninsula on Mount Samat on April 3, 1942. They concentrated their attack on the D Sector of the Orion-Bagac line, held by the Philippine Army 41st Division. The sector was breached within the first five hours of fighting, sending the 41st Division running back to the rear. Fatigue, disease, starvation, and stress had taken their toll. The men holding those sectors on the Orion-Bagac line were no longer medically able to continue fighting. Many historians describe the Fil-American defeat on Bataan as a "medical defeat" rather than a "military defeat."[1]

The 31st Infantry was told to prepare to move forward to close the gap on the line left by the rapid retreat of the 41st Division.

Phillip recalls the last counter attack. "I asked my squad leader, 'What's coming up Jess?'"

Jess said to Phillip, "I don't know, but you and I need to get up to the staff sergeant's meeting. You have to go with me. If I miss something, you'll remember something."

It was about 5 o'clock in the morning when they met under a mango tree for their commands. Phillip was already exhausted from being up all night on watch.

"Everybody from corporal to staff sergeant to platoon sergeant got their orientation for their group," Phillip said.

"The commander said, 'We are on our last push. This is our last push, in other words, we are going to make one last thrust, win or lose. Artillery will lay broads down for us. We are going up to the ridge. We have the artillery up there for us. They are going to crossfire 105s (Howitzers). Don't pay attention to it. They are on our side but they will be over our heads.'"

"Right before we dismissed our group, we were all around in a circle below the hill and we were getting our last instruction. The .30 caliber crew was to go up the center," Phillip said.

Phillip's sergeant told the unit, "If you are in the center and have to drop back down, you drop straight back down. Don't get in someone else's territory to the right or left or they might shoot you."

While the sergeant was leaning in to the group, giving instructions, Phillip heard shots fired.

"Jing! Jing! A Japanese rifle hit him right in his Adam's apple. Broke that skin. He didn't even notice it. It came across here," said Phillip, pointing to his neck.

Phillip didn't want to interrupt his sergeant, but did, "Hey Sarg, I think you are hit! Look down your shirt!"

"He was dripping right in front of us. Looks like someone just took a razor and cut that skin," Phillip said. "They let us know, they were closer than we thought. Sergeant said for us to go back to gun positions. That was at 6 o'clock in the morning. We didn't have breakfast that day. We had our last meal yesterday about 4 o'clock."

"We had to get in there and get ready for the final push. They had already outflanked us when sergeant got hit."

The crossfire began.

The 105 Howitzers were accurate and packed a powerful punch, but that didn't ease Phillip's mind.

"That is the hardest thing to be under," Phillip said. "You are walking under the artillery shells. Choo, choo, choo. Choo, choo. I remember only one fell short, but I think it was one of them ammunitions being in storage too long. I could hear it coming, just sizzling coming my way. Choo, choo, choo. Choo, choo. I didn't know which way it was coming. I didn't know where it was going to drop – fall short, beside me, fall over me. If you happened to be close by, that explosion of hot steal could burn a hole in your leg, in any part of your body."

Phillip's corporal shouted at everyone, "Hunker down, hunker down. Just keep down as low as you can."

"We were on a knoll. The Japanese were on north side and we are on the south side. We are coming up. They were coming up," Phillip said. "We were halfway to the top of that hill. They had the advantage. They were up on top looking down at us. They had the high points and they could see everything going on around there."

"We had one of those BARs (Browning Automatic Rifles) in our squad. It took a husky guy to handle that. They had a strap around his shoulder crossways. He laid down a broad brush and gave us a chance to drop back down. We were halfway up the hill at Mount Samat. We backed down and they came on down toward us. The Japanese forces broke through our front line," Phillip said.[2]

In the morning of April 9, 1942, General Edward P. King went to Lamao to surrender his forces on Bataan. In a meeting with his staff officers the night before, General King was informed that 70 percent of his men were too weak to march 100 yards, carrying their weapons. He was losing around 150 men a day to disease and starvation.

It was abundantly clear that the Fil-American II Corps side of the Orion-Bagac Line which had been breached on April 3 could not be re-established. There were gaping holes on the line which the Japanese simply poured through, and there was no hope of plugging those gaps. Efforts to establish a new and abbreviated defensive line failed as troops stumbled around the rough terrain in chaos and disarray.

At Lamao, General King told Colonel Motoo Nakayama, a staff officer for General Homma, that he had saved trucks and fuel so his men may be driven to the Japanese's desired destination. Colonel Nakayama wouldn't hear of any conditions. General King asked if his men would be treated humanely. Through a interpreter, Colonel Nakayama said, "We are not barbarians." This was the only surrender term General King would receive. No surrender term was prepared or signed, nor was any effort made to formalize the surrender.

General King and his staff officers were then driven to the town of Balanga, Bataan where they were interrogated on the number of Japanese prisoners held by the Americans, the number of tanks and artillery pieces left on Bataan, the number of troops and artillery pieces on Corregidor, and if there existed caverns or tunnels that housed large reserves of ammunition on Bataan.

When the news spread that Major General King went to meet the Japanese to surrender his Luzon Force, the 31st Infantry buried their colors and artifacts. Some of the survivors escaped into the hills to continue resisting, but most obeyed the order to surrender to the Japanese. They then underwent indescribable, brutal abuse and humiliation on the ensuing Death March and their three-and-a-half years of captivity that followed.[3]

More than half of the 3,300 members of the 31st Infantry who were surrendered at Bataan would perish while prisoners of the Japanese.[4]

American journalist and war correspondent Frank Hewlett, who spent some time on Bataan, penned a limerick poem, "The Battling Bastards of Bataan," that came to symbolize the campaign:

> *We're the battling bastards of Bataan,*
> *no mama, no papa, no Uncle Sam.*
> *No Aunts, no Uncles, no cousins or nieces,*
> *no pills, no planes, no artillery pieces*
> *And nobody gives a damn.*[5]

1. Baldassarre.
2. Illingworth.
3. Baldassarre.
4. 31st Infantry Regiment Association.
5. Gerald Wofford, "Creek Veteran Travels to Asia to Honor Fallen," *Muscogee Nation News*, May 2014.

CHAPTER 13
CAUGHT ON THE TRAIL

The end of the fighting came on Easter week as the Japanese Imperial Army closed its ranks on the desperate American and Philippine soldiers.

"We had it. We were too weak to go on," Phillip said. "We didn't know what was going to happen next, but we had been given instructions that if Bataan fell, that all the equipment, trucks, oil and gas were to be destroyed."

"I could hear gunfire, but didn't have instructions to shoot," Phillip said. "Sergeant Cole instructed the squad to get out. He told me to pull the gun out of action. 'We're surrounded,' he told us. 'The line fell.'"

The order to destroy everything was immediately carried out.

Phillip remembers Sergeant Cole telling his men that he would not give any more orders because it was all over, "I'm not giving orders no more. It's done...done. You can pick your options. You can go out to the main road. Every man to himself. This is it. I'm not 'gonna tell you what to do."

Sergeant Cole continued, "Don't try to be a hero but try to get yourself to Corregidor if you get a chance. Try and make it to Mariveles mountains for refuge."

Corregidor is an island located at the entrance of Manila Bay. The island housed a tunnel system with an underground hospital, bombproof shelters, storehouses and the Allied command center. As long as the island remained in American hands, the Japanese would be denied use of Manila Bay.

"I am going to Mariveles area and see if I can get across to the bay area," Phillip told his gun crew.

Phillip looked at Eddie and told him, "I am going to try to get to Corregidor."

Phillip and Eddie grabbed Army rations from an overturned truck. Eddie grabbed the gun and they took off, trying to make it to Corregidor, located two miles across the water from the Mariveles mountain range.

This was the last time they were together.

It took what seemed like two days for Phillip to get out of the jungle.

After traveling all night, Phillip came upon 75 GIs preparing to eat one gallon of corned beef hash. Everyone was to take just a spoonful of hash until all the soldiers had one bite. Then they would start over for a second round. Phillip was about sixth in line to eat his spoonful of corned beef hash, but he would never get his chance.

"The first guy picked up a spoon and that's it," Phillip said.

Blllllllrrrrrr. Blllllllrrrrrrr. Blllllrrrrrr.

"We were surrounded by Japanese."

"Boy, we hit the ground," Phillip said. "We all went in different directions. That corned beef hash was still sitting there. We didn't get to eat that corned beef hash. We just opened it. I think those Japanese probably ate it."

"Everything's falling. Limbs falling. They had .50s somewhere pretty close 'cause they just raked over us. It had to be .50s because them limbs were falling. They were cutting those limbs down."

Phillip told the guy closest to him to stay put, "Don't you stick your head up. They have .50s. They are spraying us with .50s."

Warning the guy a second time, Phillip yelled at him, "I said, 'Stay put!'"

"While I was lying there, I took everything out of my billfold. I took pictures I had in my wallet and took them out. I wasn't married then. I looked at pictures I had of my nieces, my nephews, and my sis Sophie."[1]

Sophie was two years older than Phillip. She was of medium height and always had shoulder-length hair. Phillip was small in stature, but he was tough. He was strong. And although the siblings were separated after their mom and grandmother died, they kept in contact throughout their boarding school years, while he was at Haskell Institute, and during the war as best they could by writing letters.[2]

"I remember telling my sis not to forget me," Phillip said. "She said she would write and I'd tease her not to send postcards."

So, the two almost always wrote letters. Phillip loved getting letters from his sister. She would cherish his letters. The two were close despite Sophie being quite the disciplinarian of the two. She was strong-willed, as was Phillip. They had to be, having survived their childhood without parents and the loss of so many family members.

Phillip had to draw upon those independent survival skills like never before.

"I dug a hole where I was laying and put the whole billfold in there and covered it up," Phillip said. "I just had to bury my billfold. I didn't want them to get my photos. I just kept my Baby Ben pocket watch."

"I thought about making a run for it, but I recalled my faulty ammunition. All I had were those .45's. I thought about those clips. If we had went for it, I wouldn't be here today. But I didn't want them to take me."

"I didn't make it," Phillip said. "I was caught on the trail with about 75 other soldiers heading for the mountains."

"I was captured."

"I got caught on the trail at 10 o'clock in the morning. The Japanese didn't treat me any different because I was Native American. Didn't matter. Didn't matter. As long as we were under the American flag, we were still their enemy."

Searching everyone, the Japanese immediately confiscated the GI's rifles and personal valuables. They took Phillip's Baby Ben pocket watch.

"I thought to myself, 'Big deal. It wasn't worth much.' They took it off me and just grinned like a possum," Phillip said. "They had us outnumbered 10 to 1 so I stood there. They took everything we had. They took jewelry. They took rings soldiers wore. If they couldn't slip it (the ring) off, they'd cut your finger off. They slapped us around. They took my .45."

"One Japanese was dumb enough to look down that barrel," Phillip said. "Do you know he had a finger on that trigger? He pulled that lever down and he took off the safety. Boom! Blowed his head off! Right there in front of us. That blood splattered. Wow. None of us did it. He did it himself."

"They did take the peninsula," Phillip said. "But they paid dearly for it."[3]

The Imperial Army believed it would be better to die with a sword in your hand than to surrender. They considered it a total disgrace for a soldier to surrender instead of dying for one's cause or leadership. They looked down upon the prisoners and didn't consider them worthy of being called warriors.[4] Also, the Japanese planned to capture the Philippines in 50 days. After 150 days, they were still fighting on Bataan. The Japanese had not yet captured Corregidor and the units in the Southern Islands. They were successful with their lightning assaults in Malaya, Indonesia, and other fronts, where they quickly overwhelmed much larger British and Dutch forces. On Bataan, they were stuck for months, unable to move forward. They received much consternation from their commanders in Tokyo and were enveloped in shame for their failure to accomplish their mission in the desired length of time.

The Japanese knew that in spite of winning the campaign on Bataan, they had lost the propaganda advantage of being regarded as an unstoppable superior force. A garrison of diseased and starved, poorly equipped and poorly trained Americans, and Filipinos, stopped them for more than 150 days. They were no longer the supermen they once believed they were. The myth was no longer credible.[5]

> "Our war — our own little rat trap
> The hopeless defense of Bataan
> A rear guard with no main body
> But a thorn in the flesh of Japan."
>
> *From "Vindication" by Lt. Henry G. Lee*[6]

1. Illingworth.
2. Taryole, Kenneth. Interview by author. Personal interview. Okmulgee, Oklahoma, June 2014.
3. Illingworth.
4. Moyer, Moe. Interview by author. Taped interview. Norman, Oklahoma, September 2014.
5. Baldassarre.
6. "Vindication" by Lt. Henry G. Lee.

CHAPTER 14
THE BATAAN DEATH MARCH

Many prisoners of war endured the worst part of their captivity during transport from the battlefield to prison camp. Few suffered more than the defenders of the Bataan Peninsula in the Philippines during the Second World War. Approximately 10,000 American soldiers, along with 62,000 Filipinos were forced to surrender to Japanese authority on April 9, 1942. Having already survived months of rough fighting on minimal rations, they were scarcely prepared for the ordeal that lie ahead.[1]

Following his capture, Phillip was taken to Mariveles. The place where he previously tried to find transportation for his escape to Corregidor now became the start of a 62-mile march that the men often referred to as "The Hike," but later came to be known as "The Bataan Death March."

At Mariveles, along with about a hundred other men, he was put into a column, four abreast and ordered to march north, along Bataan's East Road. This would mark the beginning of three-and-a-half years of hard labor, starvation, exposure to diseases, imprisonment, and inhumane abuse for this young Creek soldier, as well as thousands of American and Filipino soldiers."[2]

The first two columns began their march north on the East Road, later that evening. Most of the men marched from Mariveles, Bataan to San Fernando, Pampanga. Some began from the western town of Bagac, others from Cabcaben and yet others joined in from other points on the East Road. The conditions on the march varied from one marching column to another and the strictness of the guards varied as well. Some guards simply wanted to get the men to their destinations as quickly as possible, so they made them march at an accelerated pace, leaving little time for rest, food, or water. For the men who were already sick before they began the March, this proved to be fatal. Many would just give up and fall over the side of the road. In some of the other columns, the guards were indescribably sadistic, seeking to extract revenge in the most heinous ways on the defenseless POWs for their fallen and disgraced comrades.

The prisoners were humiliated, beaten, used for bayonet practice, run over by vehicles, decapitated, given only water which was unsafe to drink, and marched relentlessly in the Philippine heat without rest until they collapsed from exhaustion. Their lives would be ended with a quick thrust of a bayonet. For many of those POWs, the March was a chaotic jumble of the cruelest ambivalent events. The American and Philippine soldiers were denied everything – even the smallest visage of honor among soldiers. Many POWs chose suicide, doing things which they knew would get them killed by the guards or jumping off of steep ravines or bridges, as these opportunities presented themselves.

In most previous encounters, this wasn't the manner in which prisoners were treated. Military annals would later record, to the shock of the civilized world, the brutal intensity and the unspeakable treatment that the American and Philippine soldiers would suffer on their march to the prisoner of war camp. These atrocities would also later bring shame to Japan and dishonor to General Homma. He was to be executed on April 3, 1946 – ironically, on the same day he began his assault on Bataan four years earlier.

The Death March was a series of marches, which lasted from five to nine days. The distance a captive had to march was determined by the location on the trail where the captive began the horrific journey.[3] The stench of death had already permeated the peninsula and while Phillip was marching down to Mariveles village, he couldn't stand the overbearing, foul odor of decaying bodies.

"The odor was strong. I had been around animals in Oklahoma and the odor is strong when animals die, but this odor was worse," Phillip said. "When we came into Mariveles, oh, that was terrible. There were a lot of civilians – some elders, some children. You can see the bones laying there, just smoldering in those little huts. They started to decay."

"We walked right through that local village. We were herded like cattle down the hot and dusty road," Phillip said. "It was a guarded trail, one guard on each side and in the back. I thought, 'What the hell is going to happen now?' I had been marching about two hours coming down through the village and then got on that main road."

At Mariveles, there was a little school house with an artesian pipeline and the water ran continuously. Phillip tried to get a drink of water but his efforts were fruitless. He would later be denied water, food, rest, and protection from the sun.[4]

Many on the march had surrendered sick and malnourished, causing thousands to die before they reached their destination of Camp O'Donnell. How many men died on the Death

March will never accurately be known. Rough estimates put American deaths at 600 or 700; Filipino deaths somewhere between 5,000 to 10,000.[5]

"On the march, I remember one guy named Rivera. He was a Spanish boy from California and they threw him in there with the Filipino Army and he was in a truck over there where the Filipinos are," Phillip said. "I don't know where they were taking him."

"He was in a truck and he hollered my name, called me Coonie."

"I looked over there and said, 'Rivera, Is that you?'"

Rivera answered Phillip, "Yeah. Tell him I'm not in the Filipino Army. Tell them I am with you. We came over together."

Phillip told Rivera, "I don't have anything to do with that."

Rivera begged Phillip to speak for him.

"Well, I'll try," Phillip said. "That's all I can do."

"I went up to that Jap guard. I got pretty close to the guard. The guard told me to get out of there. I didn't get Rivera. He kept waving," Phillip said. "They (Japanese) really beat them (Filipinos) up. They really slapped those Filipinos around because they were fighting with us."

Phillip tried not to draw attention to himself. The captives were instructed not to assist each other, but he couldn't resist lending a helping hand. He was in the back of the pack when he started the treacherous journey and there was one Filipino scout about Phillip's size who was trying to walk along with the American prisoners. The scout's ankle was swollen and Phillip tried to help him walk. One of the Japanese guards saw Phillip helping the scout and made him let go of the wounded Filipino.

"I helped him along a half-a-mile hanging on my shoulder. He was just hobbling along on one foot. I knew he wasn't going to make it. I tried to tell them his leg was hurt, he could barely walk," Phillip said.

Phillip told the scout, "I will have to let you go."

"A few minutes later I heard a shot. I didn't look back. They killed him. I thought I better just stay to myself."

"They killed a lot of Filipinos, Americans too," Phillip said. "If they didn't like the way you look or something, they'd take you outside of the road and put a shell behind your head and kill people mercilessly for no reason at all. Just because we killed a lot of theirs, I guess."

"It's hard to think about the unmerciful killings and the boiling sun beating down on us," Phillip said of the horror after horror that he and the other soldiers endured. "Many of the soldiers' minds just snapped. They couldn't take it anymore and many died."

"They just needed to pick on somebody to slap around," Phillip said. "I got slapped around. I was supposed to be on the outer flank. That's where all the problems were. They just come up and slap you. They would hit those on the outside more."

The Japanese would do cruel things to Phillip on the march. They would back hand him, slapping him on one side of the face and then back again just for meanness, just for torment.

Phillip often asked, "What did I do? What did I do?"

Not knowing what he did to receive this treatment often brought back thoughts of his childhood.

"I didn't have much when my mother died, as far as toys went," Phillip said. "I had neighbors who had toys. I'd go over to their house and play with his toys. But he'd get to where he wanted to quit playing and he would pick up his toys. He was tired of playing, and wouldn't say anything but just pick them out of my hand and put them away. And I didn't know what to do."

Phillip would ask his friend, "What did I do? What did I say?"[6]

Phillip would eventually get in the middle of the pack and stay behind one of the taller soldiers. He found relief from the sun in the shadow of the tall soldier. Phillip stayed behind him throughout the remainder of the march as the Japanese had taken Phillip's helmet and he didn't have protection from the sun. By this time, Phillip's hair had grown longer and also provided some much-needed relief.

"Behind us as we walked away, we would hear shots every so often. I know somebody got shot, either American or Filipino," Phillip said. "We were enemies. Even though they had the upper hand, they were still mistreating us. That Geneva international law didn't mean anything to them."[7]

The Geneva Conventions are the most important component of international humanitarian law – the body of rules that protect civilians and people who are no longer fighting, including wounded and sick military personnel and prisoners of war. Their purpose is not to stop war but rather to limit the barbarity of armed conflict. The 1929 Geneva Convention Relative to the Treatment of Prisoners of War states:

Prisoners of war are in the power of the hostile Power, but not of the individuals or corps who have captured them. They must at all times be humanely treated and protected, particularly against acts of violence, insults and public curiosity.

Measures of reprisal against them are prohibited.[8]

1.   National Prisoner of War Museum, National Park Service, Andersonville, Georgia, September 2014.
2.   Bell. "Creek Soldier Survivor of 'Death March.'"
3.   "Outline of Events."
4.   Illingworth.
5.   Ibid. National Prisoner of War Museum.
6.   Author.
7.   Illingworth.
8.   "Geneva Conventions still going strong at 60," accessed January 1, 2015, https://www.icrc.org/eng/resources/documents/interview/geneva-convention-interview-120809.htm.

"The March of Death. Along the March [on which] these prisoners were photographed, they have their hands tied behind their backs."

Photo courtesy: National Archives & Records Administration

CHAPTER 15
A FAMILIAR FACE

The prisoners' first stop on the way to Camp O'Donnell was at Limay. Upon arriving in Limay, the sun was setting and the soldiers were allowed to get water in groups of 10. It was here that Phillip would see a familiar face.

"They told us that we could get water," Phillip said. "But some who were crazed with thirst, broke rank and began to run for the water. Many died in the attempt to get the water. They were quickly clobbered, shot or bayoneted."

"When it was my turn to get up and get water, I happened to notice an Indian man that I thought I knew," Phillip said. "I went over to him and was shocked to see that it was Alex Mathews, a Pawnee Indian that I had gone to school with at Haskell Institute. It was a joyous occasion for both of us."

Phillip asked Alex, "What the hell are you doing over here?"

Alex replied, "I was going to ask you the same thing."

"I was sure glad to see someone I knew," Phillip said. "It was everybody for themselves on the march until I met Mathews. We buddied up for the rest of the march. We stuck together, even on work details."

Alex was born in Cache, Oklahoma, and reared on the windswept prairie south of the tiny town of Pawnee at a time when many in Oklahoma—boys included—were able to survive only by laboring hard for $1 a day or maybe less. A member of the Pawnee Nation of Oklahoma, Alex also attended an Indian boarding school where he learned to read and write English, and endure tough discipline.

"That experience was quite valuable in the sense that at that time Indian school was very military oriented," Alex said of his boarding school life.

Alex graduated from Glencoe High School in 1938 and attended the Haskell Institute in Kansas for two years before being offered a job with the Bureau of Indian Affairs in New Mexico. But it wasn't long after his arrival in New Mexico that he was drafted for service in the Army. He was 22.

Alex was assigned to an antiaircraft artillery outfit, Battery H of the 200th Coastal Artillery. After training at Fort Bliss, Texas, he was shipped out to Clark Air Base and then, in December 1941, onto the Bataan Peninsula. His job was to shoot down Japanese aircraft flying en route to bomb the fortified island of Corregidor.

Like Phillip, Alex drew upon the strength he developed as a boy growing up in Oklahoma during the Depression. And just like Phillip, Alex had an unshakable faith that would help him get through trying times.

"We were dazed and half-dead," Phillip said. "I lost track of time, days, and didn't even know where I was."

Alex kept encouraging Phillip, telling him, "We've got to make it through."

So the two classmates from Haskell Institute just kept walking.[1]

While on the Death March, Phillip would also draw upon the strength of his ancestors who were forced on the Trail of Tears and he would tap into the teachings of his elders like never before. Because of the training he received at the Nuyaka ceremonial ground, Phillip experienced what it was like to sweat and work hard without food because of the many times he spiritually prepared his body through the act of fasting. While some soldiers on the march were going crazy, Phillip's mind would wander back to his childhood. He could hear the songs his ancestors sang at the ceremonial ground. He drew strength and encouragement from the traditional songs that he used to dance to and the church songs he used to sing. This time he would lean on those songs to march on.[2]

1. Steve Metzer, "Bataan Remembered Death March survivor knew he would return home to Oklahoma," *Lawton Constitution*, accessed July 11, 2014, http://www.angelfire.com/nm/bcmfofnm/names/names_pu/alexmathews.html.
2. Harjo.

Phillip served on burial detail. Here is a photo depicting Allied POW burial detail.

Photo courtesy: National Archives & Records Administration

CHAPTER 16
PRISONER OF WAR CAMPS
O'DONNELL AND CABANATUAN

The two Indian buddies finally made it to San Fernando, Pampanga. That's where the Death March ended, but horror still loomed ahead.

When Phillip, Alex, and the other prisoners reached the village of San Fernando, they were hungry, exhausted, dehydrated, and craving water. They were greeted by civilians, who had compassion for the captives.

"The boys and girls rushed out to meet us with cookies in their little hands," Phillip said. "But the Japanese soldiers would draw back their bayonets and threaten the children and civilians to get away. They didn't want the Filipinos to help us. Any cookies that fell on the ground were quickly crushed beneath the boots of the Japanese, who took delight in doing this kind of thing."[1]

At San Fernando, the prisoners faced more tragedy as they were crammed into steel boxcars, around 100 per boxcar and sent to Capas, Tarlac. This 20-mile trip by rail was without mercy. The sick men were defecating on each other as they were stuffed so tightly together that those who passed out, or in some cases died, did so standing up. The heat was unbearable inside those boxcars, which were unfit for human beings. Once the doors were closed, there was no ventilation inside the cramped quarters.

"We were shoved into those boxcars and there was no room at all," Phillip said. "The train was solid packed. Like sardines, we were packed shoulder-to-shoulder. When the door was closed, the heat was unbearable and many of the soldiers passed out. A lot died from suffocation, some just died of heat stroke, and others expected it (life) to end."[2]

For Phillip and Alex, the boxcar ride seemed like an eternity. They observed fellow soldiers going crazy from the claustrophobic conditions that pushed them to the brink of insanity. "That was the first inkling I had of how the mind can deteriorate," Alex said.[3]

"When the train stopped and the side doors were opened, the men fell out like cords of wood – dead," Phillip said. "They had been dead for some time because they were bloated. It was terrible."

After they arrived in Capas, those who were still alive were once again put into columns and marched another two to three miles into Camp O'Donnell. Before the war, Camp O'Donnell was being built as a base for a Philippine Army Division. It was never finished, as the war began long before its completion.[4]

At Camp O'Donnell, 50,000 American and Filipino survivors became captives of the Japanese.[5] Haphazard shelters made of bamboo provided the only protection for the soldiers from the elements. A man's rank didn't matter at Camp O'Donnell. Officers suffered the same as enlisted men. Americans suffered just as much as Filipinos. Chaplains suffered the same as the rest. According to Alex, everybody was reduced to the same level and everything was in turmoil.[6]

Camp O'Donnell did not have the sanitation infrastructure or water supply necessary to hold such a large amount of men. Many died from diseases they had since Bataan. Many caught new diseases while at the camp. There was little medicine available to the prisoners. Their inadequate diets also contributed to high death rates. Diseases such as dysentery, from a lack of safe drinking water, and beriberi, from malnutrition, were common among the POWs. The Japanese soldiers continued to murder and mistreat their captives.[7] They wouldn't allow the various Christian, social, or charity groups from Manila to bring food and medicine into Camp O'Donnell. They gave the excuse that the humanitarian groups might be guerrillas trying to sneak weapons into the camp. The trucks with life-saving supplies were told to return to Manila.[8]

During his time at Camp O'Donnell, Phillip served on bridge detail, burial detail, and water detail. He'd be out during the day and was on the move all the time. He remembers the compassion the Filipino women had for the POWs, wanting to give them fresh fruit. After receiving consent from the Japanese guards, the Filipinos often brought the soldiers a rarity – fresh fruit, usually mangos, as the months of April and May were the time of the year the mangoes were harvested in the Philippines, so they were in abundance. From that time on Phillip volunteered for detail, because it meant he would get to eat fresh fruit.

"Everybody seemed to be quiet at the camp," Phillip said. "We all were hurting. We were all thirsty. We were hungry all the time."

An average meal consisted of rice, seaweed, sweet potatoes (camotes) and dry dilis, which Phillip said resembled
little minnows. Filipinos would fry those little fishes until
they were crispy and eat them like French fries. Although
hunger took its toll on Phillip, losing 50 pounds from his
already small frame that took him from 140 to 90 pounds,
his body craved water.

"You have to have water in your system," Phillip said. "You
can go hungry for a few days, but you have to have water.
We got water at Camp O'Donnell which felt pretty good. I
was on that water detail. We'd go get that water and bring
it to them so everyone could have a drink of water. We had
enough water to take a little bath. But we needed it more
for drinking to keep from being dehydrated."

Although Phillip was at Camp O'Donnell a short time, he
often found himself reflecting about his young life in which
he graduated from Haskell just the year before. He was
having a good time on campus, falling in love with Helen,
and learning a trade where he could work with his hands.
Now, he was faced with a lot of challenges.

And one of those challenges was giving his fallen comrades
a proper burial. Phillip was on burial detail at Camp O'Donnell as was his buddy Alex. The two young Indians from
Oklahoma and other POWs tried to give their comrades a
decent burial, but could only manage to wrap the bodies in
elephant grass for interment.

"They were dying so fast in a day's time when we got to
the camp," Phillip said. "We tried to give the men the most
decent burial we could. But then it got down to where we
had to bury them 10 at a time in one grave. That's the
hardest thing to do."

Among the soldiers who died at the camp was one of Phillip's buddies who went over to the Philippines with him as a raw recruit.

"I'll never forget him – (Archie) Homer Rice from Kokomo, Indiana. He made a gunner too and we were kind of proud of ourselves. He called me Philly all the time. He was left handed. I used to call him Leftie. I gave him the Indian name, Wrong Hand."

Phillip recalled a promise the two made while at Camp O'Donnell.

Leftie approached his Oklahoma buddy with a question-like voice, "Philly?"

Phillip asked Leftie, "What is it Homer?"

Leftie told Phillip, "If we ever get out of this I want you to come to Kokomo, Indiana, and spend a week with me. And when you go back to Oklahoma, I'll come back with you. I'll stay with you awhile."

"Yeah, I'd be glad to," Phillip answered.

"I will be glad to meet your folks," Leftie said.

"I don't have no folks," Phillip replied. "I've been an orphan most of my life."

"That's okay, I'll meet your mother's sister," Leftie said.

Phillip told Leftie, "You can meet her and I have some uncles too."

"Don't forget you go home with me first and then I'll go home with you," Leftie said.

The two buddies shook hands on that promise.

But the promise was never realized as Leftie died in Camp O'Donnell, on April 29, 1942. Malaria was listed as his cause of death.

"He didn't come back," Phillip said.[9]

Camp O'Donnell had become like a tropical petri dish of diseases. There were mini epidemics that would break out at the camp and the Japanese were getting sick too. On June 2, 1942, the Japanese shut down Camp O'Donnell and moved almost everyone east to Cabanatuan Prison Camp in Central Luzon, except for about 500 men. Some men were too sick to move to the new camp. And some were left behind to help bury 1,200 men. Phillip and Richard Gordon, a staff sergeant with the 31st Infantry, company F, 2nd Battalion, were two of those on burial detail.[10]

As exhaustion, disease, and starvation killed many men each day, the Japanese presented American supply officer and medical doctor Captain Wilson with a "present."

The present: a sack of cement; the command: "Now, courtesy of Imperial Japanese Army, you make a shrine for men who die."[11]

In memory of their fallen comrades and in defiance of the Japanese (who no doubt expected a Shinto shrine) the Americans built a cement cross. Fittingly, the inscription did not contain the word "prisoner," reflecting the men's refusal to concede anything to their captivity.

The prisoners decided a cross would be best to honor the memory of their dead. They chose a cross because it was simple and easy, and they were under the impression if they built something right away, they could move to Cabanatuan. They worried that if they stayed in Camp O'Donnell any longer, they would die as well.

Phillip recalled gathering bailing wire and anything he could find to contribute to the construction of what would become known as the Sack of Cement Cross.

"They gave us one bag of cement to make that cross," Phillip said. "One of the guy's dads was in the contract business and he watched his dad build forms. He directed us, saying, 'You guys get me some scraps, nails, boards, anything you can find and I'll build the form. It don't matter if the board has nails in it, we'll get it out. Get barbed wire fence too. We can use that to get the form to where it sets. We can use it to hold the boards together.'"

"We got all the scraps. We got the material together," Phillip said. "All kinds of pebbles, any size, didn't matter. We just piled it up there and he built the form in about a day."[12]

In June 1942, the POWs erected a six-foot cement cross of perfect proportion in honor of their comrades. The base of the cross was etched by a POW's finger with the following words:

> *IN MEMORY*
> *of the*
> *AMERICAN DEAD*
> *O'DONNELL WAR PERSONNEL ENCLOSURE*
> *1942*
> *OMNIA PRO PATRIA [All for Country]*

Approximately 1,600 Americans died in Camp O'Donnell. Almost 20,000 Filipinos died in their first four months of captivity, in the same camp.[13] Camp O'Donnell went from being a prison camp to a quartermaster camp where the Japanese kept their supplies.

Surviving Camp O'Donnell for two months, Phillip was then taken in June 1942 to Camp Cabanatuan. Meanwhile, Corregidor had fallen to the Japanese and the tumult of the war continued. The POWs from the Battle of Corregidor were also diverted to Cabanatuan, making it the largest POW camp in the Philippines.

At Camp Cabanatuan, Phillip would succumb to dry beri-beri and malaria. He would also experience a great loss as it was the last time he would see his Cherokee buddy, Jacob Cornsilk.

"I hadn't seen Jacob since we were on the front lines," Phillip said.

"I was sick with malaria and it was there that I saw Jacob. He found me and asked if he could borrow my little New Testament. Each soldier was given one when they went into the service. They became precious to us. Jacob lost his, so I gave him mine. He thanked me and left."

"I never saw him again," Phillip said.

Because Phillip was afflicted with malaria, his last conversation with Jacob was brief.

"I never had malaria in my whole life," Phillip said. "I had medical attention all the time when I was in school, but I didn't take enough treatments for it (malaria). Medicine was getting low and mosquitos were so bad over there."

"It is in your blood stream. I didn't know that. I kind of felt funny. It's an awful feeling," Phillip said. "Malaria works on your mind. Your mind would kind of come and go, like you are day dreaming, sitting and sleeping. You kind of loose yourself, wondering, 'Where am I? What happened?'"

The doctor told Phillip that a lot of guys born in the city who got malaria would often suffer from relapse. Phillip tended to agree with the doc's theory.

"A lot of boys in the rural area are subject to a lot of things because of outdoor life and you are better to cope with conditions," Phillip said. "With city life, if you get cold, you go in the house. Country boys. If we got cold, we'd have to go cut wood and build a fire and cook with it. I was kind of a country boy."[14]

Country boys tended to have much better immune systems. This was also true about the "dhobies," the name given to Americans who were in the Philippines for many years before the war. Their immune systems were comparable to that of the Filipinos.[15]

As Phillip got better, he returned to burial detail. And while on burial detail, Phillip noticed a dog tag hanging on a cross.

"I just happened to be on burial detail and I just happened to pick up one of the dog tags hanging on one of the crosses on a grave," Phillip said. "I turned it over and read it."

"It was Jacob."

"It seemed like I didn't even have the urge to go on after I saw that," Phillip said.

Jacob died of dysentery on September 28, 1942. His remains were never identified.

Time passed agonizingly slow for the POWs at Camp Cabanatuan and Phillip's sadness continued on into winter.

"We were at Camp Cabanatuan at Christmas and we looked forward to the Red Cross boxes," Phillip said. "But we received very little."

Then in January 1943, some of the POWs were sent to the town of Lipa in Batangas Province. Using only the crudest and most basic hand tools, the Japanese forced them to build an airfield for their air force. This was a clear violation of the Geneva Convention, as POWs should not be forced to work to assist the enemy's war effort. The airfield was completed and used by the Japanese Air Force.

When the U.S. forces returned to liberate the Philippines in late 1944, that same Lipa, Batangas airfield was one of the fiercely contested battles, as the U.S. forces felt a great need to capture that functional air field. Today, that airfield is still being used by the Philippine Air Force. It was at Lipa where Phillip would come close to dying.

In addition to the painting courses he took at Haskell Institute, Phillip also took a class on shoe repair. He could take a shoe apart and fix it like new in no time. He was placed on shoe repair detail at Lipa when two Americans on the same detail escaped and Phillip was blamed.

"We were calling out our assigned numbers in Japanese, as we did each morning, and when they didn't call their numbers, they came after me," Phillip said.

Although he proclaimed innocence, Phillip was interrogated and whipped. The Japanese were adept at administering the Oriental sun torture – prolonged and unprotected exposure to the full glare of the sun – and Phillip was forced to kneel in a circle where he was beaten continuously all day long, subjected to capricious cruelty and abuse.

His buddies feared for Phillip's life, afraid the guards would behead him.

"I never saw those guys (again). But, if I did I wouldn't strike at them, I'd let them have a piece of my mind," Phillip said. "That's the closest I came to losing my life."[16]

1. Illingworth.
2. Illingworth.
3. Metzer.
4. Baldassarre.
5. National Prisoner of War Museum.
6. Metzer.
7. "Outline of Events."
8. Baldassarre.
9. Illingworth.
10. Baldassarre.
11. National Prisoner of War Museum.
12. Illingworth.
13. "Outline of Events."
14. Illingworth.
15. Baldassarre.
16. Illingworth.

CHAPTER 17
HELLSHIPS

In September 1944, the POWs were transferred to Camp Murphy, east of Manila, where they were met with resentment from other GIs. The American soldiers there resented Phillip and others arriving from Lipa as more POWs meant more restrictions and even fewer rations.

U.S. Navy dive bombers attacked the Japanese airfields and Camp Murphy that September, marking the first time the POWs had seen American planes in almost two-and-a-half years since the Japanese captured the Philippines. One American pilot gave Phillip and the other prisoners hope when he tipped his wing to them.

"We didn't want to get too excited because we'd get slapped around," Phillip said.

The soldiers dug a ravine and laid in it for protection. They helplessly watched as Filipino villagers were killed by bomb fire while running across the airfields.

"We were at the airfields and outside a lot," Phillip said. "You would just stop what you are doing. You just sit there until the bombing was over. They expected us to be killed with those explosives. There was always somebody saying prayers for us."[1]

As the war dragged on, more Japanese men were conscripted into the Japanese military. Japan had a shortage of men to do the heavy work in Japan. Japanese corporations began buying POWs from the Japanese Army to work in their mines, mills, and factories. This was similar to the slave trade in the Americas during the 18th and 19th centuries, where slaves were brought from Africa and sold to various plantation owners. Even the ships that transported them were reminiscent of those used in the old days of slavery.

On October 3, 1944, Phillip was shipped, with 1,100 other men, via Hong Kong on the Hellship Hokusen Maru to Formosa (now Taiwan). The Hokusen Maru sailed to northern Asia as part of a convoy of ships.

The Japanese herded the POWs into cargo ships, under very cramped and inhumane conditions for various destinations in Japan, Korea, or China. The Japanese did not mark these ships to note that there were prisoners on board. Three ships were sunk. Two of them were torpedoed by U.S. Navy submarines and one was bombed by U.S. Navy carrier based planes.

The two torpedoed ships were the Shinyo Maru, which was sunk on September 7, 1944, in Sindangan Bay, Zamboanga del Norte, in the Philippines, and the Arisan Maru, which was sunk approximately, 200 miles, southeast off Hong Kong, on October 24, 1944. On December 15, 1944, the Oryoku Maru was sunk as a result of being bombed by U.S. Navy planes, as it was anchored a mile off shore in Subic Bay, in Zambales, in the Philippines.[2]

"I was on one of the five Japanese convoy ships bound for Hong Kong," said Phillip. "The U.S. sank three of the ships in our convoy, but our ship and another survived. I can still remember the sound of our own American torpedoes coming through the water and exploding into the Japanese ships and them not knowing which ships held American prisoners."

The ship Phillip was on was also attacked. Everyone was screaming as they thought they were going to die.

"We were torpedoed, but they missed us. I could hear the hissing sound of that torpedo," Phillip said. "I was sitting up front of the ship and I could hear that whistling sound. It was a thump noise in the water, and the next thing you are going to hear is a boom. Shhhoooo, boom. That could be just it. We survived. And, I just think somebody prayed for us."[3]

While on the Hokusen Maru, Phillip was able to crouch down in a corner of the ship and stay there due to his small stature. And daily, Phillip received slight solace upon waking each morning and looking at his Pawnee buddy Alex. As Phillip looked at his former schoolmate, Alex would hold up his forefinger to indicate he was still alive. That was just enough hope for the two Indian buddies to survive another tortuous day in captivity.

Phillip was never able to shake the memory of the horrible conditions of 200 to 300 soldiers being crammed into the cargo hold of a rusty and smelly old ship.

"A lot of men died on the ships. They exposed us to be slaughtered. They didn't feed us. The conditions were like hauling cattle. The odor was strong."

"They (Japanese) were getting rid of the dead bodies by throwing them out to sea," Phillip said. "They had a trough about 10 feet long, like a hog trough. It stuck way out the side of the ship, angled about 45 degrees. They would slide them off the top there and throw them into the ocean. A lot were buried out to sea. That was sad."

Phillip saw a few men being thrown overboard. And, he was almost buried at sea. It was during one incident aboard the ship that he was presumed dead.

"At the time, I was so sick with fever, I could hardly move," Phillip said. "I remember during the night they would hoist the bodies up by a crane. I was so sick I would often pass out. It was at one point that I woke up and found myself hoisted up in the air. I remember it being a clear night with a full moon. I began to move and struggle, so they brought me down, knowing that I was still alive."[4]

Many died from bombings and torpedoes, but many more died from the inhumane conditions and criminal neglect during the course of these various journeys on board those hellships. Thirty-six men died on the Hokusen Maru's trip from Manila to Takao, Formosa, from October 3, 1944 to November 11, 1944. It was a short trip in distance, but it took many days.

In Formosa, the soldiers were briefly held at the Inrin Temporary POW Camp. "A lot of time we were outside and we were under bombardment by American B-29s," Phillip said. "You'd just stop what you are doing and sit there until the bombing was over. I never saw so much bombing."

Men were kept at Inrin while they recovered from their trip on the Hokusen Maru. Some men died in Inrin from the diseases they caught on the trip and others were too sick to continue their trip to Japan. Of the original 1,100 men who began the trip in Manila, only around 500 were able to continue the trip to their final destination in Moji, Japan. The Hokusen Maru was known to the POWs as the "Benjo Maru."

Benjo is the Japanese word for "toilet."[5]

1. Illingworth.
2. Baldassarre.
3. Illingworth.
4. Wofford, "A Native American Patriot: Phillip Coon."
5. Baldassarre.

CHAPTER 18
SLAVE LABOR

From Formosa (Taiwan), Phillip was sent to Moji, Japan, on the Hellship Melbourne Maru arriving January 23, 1945. He was then transported by train north to Kosaka and became a slave laborer at the Sendai #08B Kosaka POW Camp, mining copper for Fujita Gumi Kosaka Kozan (today's Dowa Holdings Co. Ltd.).

It was a bitter, cold January day when Phillip arrived in Japan. He arrived with the first group of POWs totaling 150. When they got off the train, they marched uphill to a plateau and passed by a school house with a white picket fence where students were playing in the school yard. The POWs continued marching down the backside of the hill to the POW camp.

The compound had a wall board fence about nine feet tall and was located atop Kosaka's highest hills, where the swirling winds made the POW camp feel even colder. Along with American soldiers, there were Dutch and British soldiers in the camp. In total, 343 POWs were held at Kosaka until the end of the war.

The prisoners arrived in what Phillip termed, "the coldest winter I have ever known." Coming from the warm tropical climate of Philippines, the men sent to Japan, Korea, and

China had to adjust to the sub-freezing temperatures of Northern Asia, without the proper personal equipment and indoor heating to survive such cold temperatures.[1]

"We arrived at the camp in January 1945 and spent a hard winter there. We lost six men at that camp," Phillip said. "Freezing to death, many laid down and never woke up. I'm glad it went that way. They just went to sleep. They were undernourished and didn't have any medication. To this day, I don't know if their families got their bodies or not."

The Kosaka Mine flourished as one of four big copper mines in Japan. Some POWs worked in the machine shops and electrical shops, and the rest worked on the mountainside in the northwest side of the camp.[2] Phillip did slave labor in a copper smelting mine, working around a steel furnace and hot slabs.

"We had the big old tongs to pull the copper slabs out and move them," Phillip said. "They were heavy. They were about a foot long, foot wide. My job was to put on another tong and put it to another area. We did manual labor in moving stuff around."

In the mines, Korean guards stood watch over the POWs. Phillip recalled that one of the guards, although he wasn't partial to the POWs, had respect for them. "He would kind of lean on our side and give us a break. He was real human to us," Phillip said of the Korean guard.

On one particular break, the half-Korean, half-Japanese guard, who did not carry a gun but carried a stick to use on them, called all American prisoners of war way back in the mine where the prisoners worked.

"Yasumi," the guard said.

Phillip looked at the guy next to him and asked, "What do you think he is trying to say?"

Before waiting for an answer, Phillip said, "I think he is trying to tell us to rest. He said, 'Yasumi.' I learned that (word) in the Philippines. I am going to ask him."

Phillip took his hand and wiped the sweat off his brow, and asked the guard if he meant for them to rest.

The guard responded, "Ah, yes."

"He took us to that tunnel to rest, way back in there," Phillip said. "The guard took a little stick, made a little wave mark (on the ground), and covered it up, saying, 'Yasumi, yasumi.'"

"We looked up at him. We're resting. He's resting too. He was trying so hard to tell us something."

"I think he is trying to tell us somebody's in the grave and he covered up the soil, but he didn't put a mound on it," Phillip said. "I reached down there and put a little mound on it. And when I did that he put a stick in it. And that is the sign that somebody was put to rest in the ground."

"Neither one of us could understand the (other's) language," Phillip said. "When he put that stick in there, I told the other guy he told us somebody died."

"All he could say was roos," Phillip said. "Somebody said roosie. I said Roosevelt. Boy, his eyes got big and he said, 'Roosevelt, ahhh.'"

"The guard was trying to say Roosevelt died," Phillip said.

President Roosevelt died on April 12, 1945.

1. "Outline of Events."
2. Sasamoto, Taiko. "POW Research Network Japan, Detailed Memo on the POW Camps," accessed December 28, 2014, http://www.us-japandialogueonpows.org/2013POWvisit/Kosaka%20Camp%20Memo.pdf.

A photo from a brochure about Kosaka, Japan.

CHAPTER 19
LIBERATION IS AT HAND

The American soldiers spent nearly six more months in the Japanese camp and the winds of fate were about to shift.

Unknown to the POWs, liberation was close at hand.

"They gave us longer breaks and we had a lot of rest. We rested for a whole week," Phillip said. "Their attitude was changing toward us day by day. Everybody sensed something was happening because of how they were treating us. I thought to myself, 'What is happening?' I didn't know we were winning the war."

"We were ordered by the Japanese officers to clean up the camp and ourselves. They told us to tidy up. We didn't know what was going on. Another two weeks passed and we still didn't have any idea that freedom was close at hand."

With little hope of liberation, the soldiers ebbed out a daily existence. The next two weeks were uneventful with the exception of what the prisoners thought was an earthquake. That "earthquake" turned out to be the atomic bomb that was dropped at Hiroshima.[1]

After three-and-a-half years of fighting daily just to stay alive, it would all soon be over for Phillip and those who survived.

The Japanese commandant came up to talk to Captain Davis of the Air Force. Later, Captain Davis called to assemble the soldiers and Phillip remembered the captain's speech.

"They think we are winning the war and things are a lot closer than we think, but that doesn't mean you get too happy and get excited. I just want you to remember one thing – each and every one of us here took an oath," Captain Davis said. "Raise your hand. You are still under oath, and so am I. Nothing has changed. You are still committed to that flag. I am too. We are still under oath. We had a hard winter here and I know we are getting impatient with each other. They told us to take a rest. We'll take advantage of that and tidy up a bit. This gives us an opportunity to get our act together and get along. We should get along. You never know, we might be ordered to get out of here. When they say let's go, be ready to go at any time."

"That captain was a West Point man," Phillip said. "He made sense. He made a pretty good, short speech."

The next morning when everyone in the camp woke up, the guards all of a sudden were gone and the double gates in front of the compound were wide open. The Japanese guards had walked away during the night and the Korean guard who was in charge was also gone.

"We woke up that morning and as the first of us looked out, we were shocked to see that the gate to the compound was wide open and that the Japanese had just walked away," Phillip said. "That same day, a Navy plane found us. Next day or so an Army airlift came with food and clothes. We began to shout and tell one another what we were going to do when we got home. Buddy was grabbing buddy saying, 'Well, it looks like we made it this far. I guess we'll make it home together after all.'"

About two hours later that morning, American airplanes began searching the camps.

"We heard an airplane in the sky," Phillip said.

Phillip described the distant noise as one that reminded him of the sound his mother and aunt's Maytag washing machine made – putt, putt, putt.

As Phillip and a couple of buddies kept standing there and looking toward the sky, they heard that sound again.

Putt, putt, putt.

"Listen to it," Phillip said. "It will go off again. We couldn't see it. We could only hear the sound. We heard that sound again."

Putt, putt, putt.

"You know it sounds like a Maytag washing machine," Phillip said. "Yeah, that's Maytag. We told the guys in the building. Maytag is coming."

They asked, "Who is Maytag?"

"You listen after a while," Phillip said. "I think they are searching those camps. Then we heard it. Putt, putt, putt."

"Then one plane came in real low," Phillip said. "It was a dive bomber. It came right over us and kept getting lower and lower. Kept circling around. Pretty soon we see that star on there."

"It was American. It tipped its wing at us and we began to shout and wave our shirts in the air. Boy, everybody was outside in the compound and some were on the roof. That's when the excitement got started."

"The pilot dropped the first aid kit down to us and his handkerchief with the words written on it: 'THE WAR IS OVER – YOU ARE GOING HOME.'"[2]

"That was a big day," Phillip said.

Excitement in the camp spread like wildfire. But just as quickly as the celebration began, sorrow swept through the compound as there was a deep sadness in each heart and a sense of loss for those who weren't present to be caught up in the thrill of going home.

After the Navy pilot dropped "THE WAR IS OVER" message, another plane dropped canned goods. There were four gallons of canned goods to a case and the cases were put into two welded drums. The drums were too heavy and the chute never opened. The drums went about a quarter of the way in the soft ground and had to be dug out.

Along with the American soldiers, there were about three members of the Black Dutch Army at the compound. "Those Dutch were busting the No.10 cans and they were eating them," Phillip said. "Captain Davis chewed them out. 'You get those up to the compound or you won't eat. I am still in charge here.'"

Captain Davis was strictly military and every morning he reminded the soldiers that they were still under oath.

"We stayed at the camp another week," Phillip said. "We

didn't work for a whole week. We stayed back and got everybody medical attention. We had one medical officer named Lieutenant Green."

The soldiers were also waiting for transportation.

"The little trains were all so small in Japan around Yokohama," Phillip said. "They had enough trains to send up there to come get us and we came on down to Tokyo. I think we rode all night in those little trains. I don't think nobody slept. We were very excited. We just wandered around the train all night."

A U.S. battleship and an English battleship were anchored in Tokyo. That's where Phillip and the other soldiers were able to send word to loved ones that they were coming home.

Remembering Helen's rural route number from when he was in school at Haskell Institute, Phillip sent word to Helen, "I left for Hawaii and I am coming back to the states."

Whether one was a WWII veteran serving in Europe or the Pacific, it might be months before they actually came back home. The trip home could sometimes take close to a year depending on the ship or when one's area was repatriated.

For Phillip, the trip home couldn't come soon enough. But before the Creek soldier headed home, he was flown back to Manila.

"I thought we would be flying home from Tokyo, but the plane started going southwest instead of east," Phillip said. "Shoot. We are not going toward Seattle. We are going another direction. They were flying us back to the Philippines. We flew back to Manila."

Phillip was in the 29th Replacement Camp, south of Manila for about eight to 10 days where he received medical attention for a boil and had a medical checkup at the dispensary, which was made up of no more than a little old tent with cots. "I got a boil on the inside of my elbow. That bothered me all the time," Phillip said. "I never had a boil in my life."

Commenting on how the boil was building up, the nurse said, "We are going to have to lance it. With the heat here, it could be infected and you could lose your arm."

The nurse instructed Phillip to take his shirt off, lie down, and turn his head the other way. "Boy, that irritated me," Phillip said. "The blood shot out of there."[3]

Once Phillip received medical attention, he would soon be going home.

Phillip was liberated in September 1945.

Out of 12,000 American soldiers and officers, and 78,000 Philippine solders, it is estimated that 650 of that number of American soldiers died on the infamous Death March; 5,200 American soldiers died at the O'Donnell Prison Camp and at Camp Cabanatuan. This number does not include those who died on unmarked Japanese prison ships that were bombed by the American submarines, nor does the death toll include the undetermined number of Americans who died in prisoner of war camps throughout Japan.[4]

1. Berryhill.
2. Bell, "Creek Soldier Survivor of 'Death March.'"
3. Illingworth.
4. Baldassarre.

CHAPTER 20
A PROMISED FULFILLED

"We came back into San Francisco about 4 p.m.," Phillip said. "It donned on me. Oh, I made that promise with Jake."

He recalled standing at the back of the ship with Jacob, watching the Golden Gate Bridge go out of sight nearly four years ago. Phillip could vividly recall Jacob saying, "When we come back, if we come back, let's come to the front of the ship. And we'll watch as that picture will come back again as we get closer."

"So I hustled and I just got up front and I stood there," Phillip said. "We came in the evening. Everybody was looking forward to it since we were gone so long. Sure enough it happened. Sure enough that picture came back in focus. All of a sudden the San Francisco Bay came into sight."

"Just like Cornsilk said, 'We'll come back and see it again.'"

"A lot of guys were shaking hands. They were whistling," Phillip said. "And everybody was screaming and hollering, 'We're home. We're home.' I sat down by myself. Jake wept that time when we left, but this time I was alone, and I had tears coming down my eyes."

"He wasn't there but I kept his promise," Phillip said. "I had the tears like he had when we left. That's one thing he asked me. We shook hands on it and I fulfilled that promised."

Although Phillip knew Jacob for a short time, he would always remember his buddy, often thinking of him when he heard the song "My Buddy," written in 1922 by Walter Donaldson.

Once the ship docked in San Francisco, the soldiers had to stay on the ship all night.

"They hooked up a motion picture and nobody even watched that movie," Phillip said. "We stayed the night on the dock in the Bay area. Nobody was on deck. We were so irritated and wanted to get off. I don't know why we spent the night there. Some that really needed medical attention were still on that ship."

"That next morning some high officials were trying to get off the ship and there was this medical officer, a major. He said, 'I don't care if you are top general of this ship you stay put and go back up the ramp. There are people on the ship who need medical attention. You just downgrade yourself to be under that flag. You just go back up that ramp. And, if they rebuke, I'll see to it that every officer on this ship would get court-martialed.' They turned around and went back up the ramp."

After getting off the ship, Phillip spent about two weeks at Letterman General Hospital in San Francisco where he got his shots and additional medical attention. He was also issued new clothes. "It was like going back to the service when we got new clothes," Phillip said.

Following his time at Letterman General Hospital, Phillip wanted to go to Denver but instead was sent to Fort Sam Houston in San Antonio, Texas. He was then transferred to Fort Bliss in El Paso, Texas, where he stayed put in Beaumont General Hospital, per doctor's orders.

"My kidneys were all fouled up," Phillip said. "I'd eat something real good, about three or four bites, and my stomach feels full. So they gave me a shot to loosen up. The doctor said, 'If you stay put, you will be all right. If you don't, you won't make it. You all have been through too much.'"

"I took my medication. I followed a lot of orders," Phillip said. "I got new glasses too that made me look like a hoot owl."[1]

By following doctor's orders, Phillip began to feel better. He was able to take leave in January 1946 when he married his high school sweetheart Helen on January 7 in Kansas City. She would be his wife for 67 years.

Phillip returned to Fort Bliss to finish out his military career. And, all the while he also kept in contact with his sister Sophie. She treasured Phillip's letters, as well as one postcard in particular of Phillip proudly sitting upon a motorcycle. Although he never owned a motorcycle, Phillip had a fascination with motorcycles and took a photo at the Bucking Bronco Photo Shop in Texas that could be used on a postcard. He wrote Sophie:

Monday nite, February 11, 1946

Hi Folks –
Here is a picture for your family. Tell all the kids hello for me.
Hope they are ok. Hope to be going toward Tulsa soon. So long – folks.

Me
Phillip

After the war was over, Sophie shared the postcard and letters with her children. Sophie's son, Kenneth Taryole, recalled how the Japanese cut out words to censor those letters. "At an early age, I remember seeing one letter and it was censored," Kenneth said. "It was odd seeing the letter cut up, but the Japanese cut out words before it was sent to my mom."[2]

1. Illingworth.
2. Taryole.

Phillip and Helen Coon on their wedding day, January 7, 1946 in Kansas City.

CHAPTER 21
A SOLDIER'S SILENT PRAYER

After the war, little was made of the plight of these men. Unknown to most, 37 percent of American POWs held by the Japanese died compared to only four percent of American POWs who died at the hands of the Germans. The death rate among the Defenders of Bataan was much higher because of their weakened condition prior to their capture. Most of the men of Bataan were sick and destitute when they entered captivity. The months of acute malnutrition and exposure to diseases had taken its toll, so they died at a much higher rate than the other prisoners of war.[1]

Approximately 1,500 men from Bataan escaped to Corregidor. Once they arrived in Corregidor, General Wainwright saw what type of condition they were in and he immediately put them into the hospital.

While the mortality rate of the camps varied widely, many POWs battled illness, faced death, witnessed suicides, or buried their closest friends. Survivors believe that denial helped them live. In the words of a survivor of the Bataan Death March, "Some survived because they never realized just how rotten the situation was. Others survived day to day—bullheaded stubbornness would be a good explanation."[2] They always knew when a buddy had given up and lost his will to live. They knew they would be burying him very soon.

When asked how he miraculously survived the Bataan Death March and prisoner of war camps, Phillip shared that he believed his faith in God had preserved him. Even when he was headed to the Philippines on the USAT Willard A. Holbrook, Phillip believed God was showing him His marvelous creation in the Pacific Ocean – so vast; so deep and blue.

In combat while dodging bullets, Phillip said prayers would bring him through the battle, "You can't beat prayers. We just ran out of food, ammunition, and men. But we didn't run out of prayer. Thank the Lord for that."[3]

"I could have been killed 10 times in the area where I was," Phillip said. "Two guys I was with one day were killed and I'm still standing."

While in the Philippines, Phillip reflected on words of wisdom from his minister, "You don't live for tomorrow, because He might not give you tomorrow. This might be your last day here. Do what you can now. Here, where you are at. Not tomorrow, because tomorrow can take care of itself. Nobody has assurance that you will have tomorrow. Time is right now where you are at. What you are doing?"

"I thought to myself, it was about time I look up and thank Him for today and what tomorrow brings," said Phillip, who had been baptized earlier at Haskell. "Let it be, whatever happens. Anything could happen. I became a Christian when I was in captivity. I surrendered my life when I was in the military. Through this, I was finally able to exercise my faith."

The Japanese didn't allow the POWs to have a religious service, but they could pray.

So, Phillip would pray.

"I prayed silently in captivity when it hit my mind," Phillip said. "I lay there with my eyes closed. We called it silent prayer. I did a lot of silent prayer."

Likewise, there were a lot of prayers said for Phillip back home.

"I got to thinking for all that I went through, someone was praying for me. In the evenings when I was at the POW camps, I would lay down to sleep and I would wonder if I would ever really know what happened to some of my buddies, but I was comforted in knowing that someone back home was praying for me. I knew it had to be, because there I was on the front lines and people were dropping to the right and to the left of me and yet, I remained unhurt."

Phillip later would tell Helen that he knew people were praying for him, and offering a lot of prayers. She told Phillip that there were several times that people would go to church on Friday night and not leave until Sunday, praying continuously for him and the other soldiers.

"My wife's folks were Christian people," Phillip said. "She told me that they would have night service up to 2 o'clock in the morning, maybe up to 3 o'clock in the morning still praying (at) interval times. They would take a break, and go back and encourage each other."

"I think back to the situation. A lot of people had prayed for us." Phillip said. "Christian people of all walks of life prayed for WWII. You just know that God had a hand in it. The Creator was looking down and seeing the situation I was going through."

In addition to prayer, Phillip also attributed his survival

to the different details that he worked while fighting for his life.

"I think that being on special detail at the camps helped me survive there because I was always moving around," Phillip said. "I just live for the day. I live for the hour where I'm at with the situation."

"Grandpa's faith was unwavering in everything that he had to endure," said Phillip's grandson Robert Coffey. "Some guys would give up and just die. They didn't have any hope. Grandpa always said as a deacon in his church to 'pray much in your life.' Prayer carried him through all he had to endure."[4]

Haskell Institute classmate Edna Pickering remembered shaking hands with Phillip and the other Indian boys from school who volunteered for service, wishing them well. "At that time I didn't realize how serious and dangerous of a time these boys were going into," Edna said. "It was bad, real bad. And I know God was with Phillip and brought Phillip back to us."[5]

Principal Chief George Tiger recalled asking Phillip how he was able to survive suffering in the Japanese prison camps. "The thing that he always shared with me was the ability to reach back and grasp the traditions and the culture that he was taught and that has been handed down to us through the generations," said Chief Tiger. "It was a testament to who we are as Indian people. As a race of people, we are always the first to answer the call, when it comes to defend the honor of this country. Even during a time when we weren't citizens of this country, we were the first to answer the call. The endurance of the Muscogee was tested on the Trail of Tears and gave today's people and its soldiers the strength to survive hardships."[6]

"Phillip is the epitome of what the world should be. Throughout his life he was a role model who overcame adversity and was still a humble person who contributed greatly to his people," said Chief Tiger. "All we have to do as Oklahomans, as Americans, is to use him when we think it is real bad in our lives and look to what he went through. It is never that bad as what he went through."[7]

1. "Outline of Events."
2. National Prisoner of War Museum.
3. Gary Fife, "Muscogee (Creek) Nation honors POWs; veterans on Memorial Day," *Muscogee Nation News*, June 15, 2012.
4. Coffey, Robert. Interview by author. Tape recording. Norman, Oklahoma, September 2014.
5. Pickering.
6. Ibid, Fife.
7. "Chief George Tiger, "Phillip Coon Eulogy" (Funeral Service, Okmulgee, Oklahoma, June 27, 2014).

CHAPTER 22
BACK ON AMERICAN SOIL

Phillip was formally discharged June 26, 1946 as a Corporal. That same month, he returned to Oklahoma where he and his wife Helen made their home in Tulsa on S. Trenton Avenue.

Soldiers who were in one of the initial groups to return to the U.S. were welcomed home especially if they returned to a major city. But if they lived in the south or didn't live in a big city, they got off the ship and went home and got a job.[1]

That's what Phillip did. He took on odd jobs. He also attended night classes on commercial art and received on-the-job training working with various painting contractors. He loved to work with his hands and he was not afraid of hard work.

"I really wanted to be a sign painter when the war ended, but I became a commercial painter," Phillip said. "I stuck with that and learned that trade."

Phillip became employed by Fifth and Boston Corporation as a painting foreman. He was a member of the Local Union #1895 Painters and Decorators of America. As a union painter he did high-scaffolding work. He wasn't afraid of heights and painted many of Tulsa's city skyscrapers. Phillip liked the high-scaffolding work because it paid more. He would work until his retirement in 1981.

Phillip's Army buddies Ed Beyuka and Alex Mathews also came home. Ed became an accomplished silversmith and Alex went on to serve as Chief of the Pawnee Nation of Oklahoma.

Sports continued to play an important part in Phillip's life. Helen equally enjoyed sports, particularly basketball. She said when she played basketball, she jokingly considered herself to play like Charles Barkley, one of the National Basketball Association's most dominating power forwards. Not to be outdone by Helen, Phillip would compare his athletic ability to one of the greatest heavyweight boxers, Muhammad Ali. Phillip, too, had a way of stinging his opponents.

In the 1970s, Phillip started a fast pitch men's softball team called the Tulsa Indians. Years later, he would watch more softball games than suit up to play. One day, while watching a softball tournament at the Wetumka Sucker Day Festival, Phillip was asked to play for the Oklahoma Scramblers so they could actually field a team. It was August when the temperature in Oklahoma is usually above 100 degrees. On this particular day, the temperature topped 106 degrees.

"Our team only had eight players. We were a real Indian team, always short of players. The umpire would not let us play with eight players," Chief George Tiger said. "We looked up in the stands and saw Phillip. I asked Dink Bemo, 'What do you think, should I ask Phillip?'"

"It wouldn't hurt," said Dink, a member of the Seminole Nation and coach of the Scramblers.

Phillip jumped at the chance to play. "Yeah, I want to play," he said. "But give me a minute."

He went to his car, opened his trunk and changed into his baseball uniform – an old-time wool baseball uniform. At 106 degrees, it was too hot for wool, but that didn't stop Phillip.

"We won the game 1-0," Chief Tiger said. "Phillip got a hit and scored the winning run, and Helen was there cheering him on."

Phillip scored another win in 2005 when he was inducted into the Haskell Hall of Fame for his athletic ability for both baseball and basketball. He was honored by family, friends, and fellow veterans who surprised him with a Hall of Fame ceremony and presented him with a Prisoners of War and Missing in Action framed poster.

Helen was always by Phillip's side, whether he was playing sports or being honored. However, Phillip would be the first to say Helen was his world. They had tough times, but they were a truly happy, loving family. They were often seen walking hand and hand, and Phillip was a true gentleman, always opening doors for Helen.

Helen was there one step behind him or beside him. Theirs was a marriage made in heaven.

Phillip would tell you his faith in God and love for his family got him through the war. He would also say that Helen served as a source of strength.

Helen lived a lifetime of dedicated service to the church and its work. She ministered to the needs of people, particularly the youth and served as Sunday school director. Helen was the Women's Missionary Union Director for the Muscogee-Wichita-Seminole Baptist Association, having been involved with the work of the association since 1948. As director, Helen's service involved extensive travel throughout the country, as well as international travel to such places ironically as Japan, Canada, and the Bahamas. She sang with the Native Praise choir, teaching young leaders in the church to sing and lead Creek songs. She traveled with Native Praise to Nicaragua and England.

She also worked as a caseworker for the Creek Nation Child Welfare Program.

"Whether I'm involved as a caseworker working toward the physical and emotional welfare of my clients or if I'm involved in the spiritual welfare of those in the church association, I'm still helping people, particularly the youth, and that makes both my jobs go hand-in-hand," Helen said. "Both are rewarding."[2]

She, along with Phillip, would help many young people through their work for the church. They were members of the Little Quarsarty Indian Baptist Church near Cromwell, Oklahoma. Later, they would join Little Cussetah Baptist Church, which was closer to their home in Sapulpa.

"I remember Phillip and Helen came to our church at Little Cussetah and they wanted to join our church," said Edna Pickering, who became a lifelong friend of the family. "They were really good workers for the Lord, him and her both. They would go to people's homes. They would go to the hospital, visiting the sick."

Phillip taught an all-Creek Sunday school class. Those who attended his class spoke their Creek language and sang their songs in Creek. Phillip enjoyed teaching the class. He loved to sing and although he would hardly ever lead the singing, he would lead his favorite Creek song "Vm Vnicvs." In English, it translates to "Help Me To Pray."

Vm Vnicvs
"Help Me To Pray"

Chorus:
Vm vnicvs! Vm vnicvs!
Help me! Help me!
Emekusapkvn vm vnicvs!
Help me in prayer!

1. Cv'nokkiket wakkiyof,
   When I lay in sickness,
   Cv'nokkiket wakkiyof,
   When I lay in sickness,
   Cv'nokkiket wakkiyof,
   When I lay in sickness,
   Vm vnicvs.
   Help me.

[Chorus]

2. Cv'stemerket huerlyof,
   When I stand suffering,
   Cv'stemerket huerlyof,
   When I stand suffering,
   Cv'stemerket huerlyof,
   When I stand suffering,
   Vm vnicvs.
   Help me.

[Chorus]

3. Cv'lvrvnet wakklyof, etc.
   When I lay near death, etc.

4. Cesvs hvlwe liketskat, etc.
   Jesus who lives in heaven, etc.

5. Cv'rke hvlwe liketskat, etc.
   My Father in heaven, etc.

6. Mekusapvlke toyatskat, etc.
   You Christians, etc.

Phillip also found time for church socials, especially when there was a softball game involved.

"They used to play softball on the church grounds and we would go out to the ball park after church," said Edna. "When it was time for Phillip to bat, he rolled up his pants and he had his tennis shoes on. He was acting like he was Babe Ruth, swinging that bat like a big shot."

Helen would yell, "Hit it Phillip."

"Helen and I, and the other ladies were sitting on the bench watching the men play," Edna said. "There must have been too many ladies sitting on the bench, as that bench fell over and we all fell to the ground laughing."

The monthly church socials were a lot of fun. Following the softball game, everyone would go to the arbor for chips and hot dogs.[3]

In the Creek church the men sit on the left side of the church with the deacons sitting on the front row and the women would sit on the right side with the women leaders sitting in the front. The men and women didn't sit together. "That's just the way the elders did back then," said Phillip's son Michael. "A lot of our churches are so small and they still go by the tradition of the men on the left and the women on the right."

Sitting on the men's side, Phillip would have his Bible out. He'd have his pencil and paper.

"Thinking shouldn't he be listening to the preacher, I would wonder what he was doing" Edna said. "And, after the church was over, he would take the scripture and give it to certain ones in church to read when they had time. I knew Phillip knew the Bible and he would take time to talk with me if there was something I didn't understand."

Phillip was also head of the Royal Ambassadors, a mission discipleship organization for boys in grades one through six. However, the church was so small that they included both elementary and high school boys.

"Every Wednesday night you could find Phillip at the church and he taught the young boys about the Bible," Edna said. "He had time for these young boys. He would take them camping and take them to Falls Creek for summer church camp (in Davis, Oklahoma). He would always say, 'Remember to always pray, always pray and the Lord will bring you through.' He was a good role model for these boys. He captivated them. Many went into the military and many went into the Lord's service because of Phillip."

Phillip was a mentor to so many young men. One of those young men was David Foster. David's first encounter with Philip was at the church Christmas program. David played baby Jesus, and Phillip and Helen portrayed Joseph and Mary.

As David grew up, he became involved in the Royal Ambassador program and Phillip became his mentor.

"I didn't realize he was a prisoner of war," David said. "I was just always amazed that he was my mentor. He always told us to believe in prayers. He taught us Creek hymns, took us camping, and taught us to tie knots. If we didn't tie the knot right, we'd have to tie it over and over again."

"This man had been through so many things and he would

tell us to pray much. I believe that's what got him through the war and back home. He taught us to have respect for others by having joy in your heart and a smile on our face when meeting somebody," David said. "He was just a wonderful man with the love of the Lord in his life."

Phillip was always willing to lend a hand to help David. He would give him tools, take him out to eat, or give him some extra money.

"I never asked for anything," David said. "Mr. Coon was just always giving and willing to do anything."

A grown man, David is now a grandfather and he teaches the Royal Ambassadors. In taking over the Royal Ambassador program David had the name of their chapter changed to the Phillip Coon Chapter, in honor of his mentor.[4]

Phillip would serve as a mentor to his own father. Phillip always considered himself an orphan after his dad dropped him off at Euchee Boarding School. But years later, Phillip's dad returned to his life. Phillip loved his father, but didn't want to grow up and be an alcoholic like him. Phillip's positive influence on his dad led him to the Lord, and it was a wonderful sight for Phillip to see his dad sitting under the shade tree at his house reading the Bible.

1. Harrison, John, and Fran Harrison. Interview by author. Personal interview. Americus, Georgia, September 2014.
2. Kathryn Bell, "CN Employee Sees Reward In Serving Others," *Muscogee Nation News*, August 2001, 5.
3. Pickering, Edna. Interview by author. Taped interview. Norman, Oklahoma, November 2014.
4. Foster, David. Interview by author. Taped interview. Norman, Oklahoma, January 2015.

CHAPTER 23
A DIFFICULT TRANSITION

The memories of war, torture, and death remained vivid in the mind of the former 31st Infantry gunner, which made coming back home a difficult and tough transition for Phillip. One could see the scars of war in his eyes. He had what some would say is a typical WWII prisoner of war mentality. He was not a man who needed to speak. He was extremely reserved and humble.[1]

For years, he wouldn't wear or use anything unless it said "Made in the USA."[2] And, like so many veterans, he felt used by his country especially in the 50s and 60s.[3] He would only tell Helen of the inhumane treatment and horrors he experienced in the Philippines and Japan. He had a short temper at times, brought on by what he endured in battle, on the Death March, and as a former prisoner of war.

It was not until after the Vietnam War, in the middle 1970s, that this condition would be diagnosed as Post Traumatic Stress Disorder or PTSD. Phillip and the other former prisoners of the Japanese never received the proper treatment they needed after their ordeal. They were undiagnosed and untreated. PTSD is caused by long-term exposure to very stressful and horrific situations. Its symptoms include flashbacks, anxiety attacks, a sudden burst of anger, paranoia, insomnia, violent nightmares, and eating disorders. Along with PTSD, many of these men were also suffering from the effects of acute malnutrition, which affected them psychologically, as well as physically.[4]

"My nerves are bad," Phillip wrote on his VA medical form 40 years after the war. "I get upset over small matters. My nerves have been getting the best of me. Sometimes occasionally, I still have horrible dreams that I am still in captivity. I have been sleeping in bed alone. I wake up at nights, my feet jerking. I still experience hot flashes on my feet. My legs are not in too good shape."

Sophie's son Kenneth remembers when his uncle came back home from overseas and the stress he was under. "I was about five or six years old," Kenneth said. "I remember going to their house and I remember my brother reaching across the table for something. Uncle Phillip slapped at my brother's hand, yelling at him, 'Ask for it and don't reach for it!' I didn't expect that. I was kind of nervous and I guess as a little boy, I thought he was mean and I was kind of scared of being around him. I suppose some of those emotions from war were coming into play. But at a young age though, I didn't realize that we had a hero in our family. It is still hard to believe there is a hero in our family."[5]

Phillip and Helen had four children – Chester, Jeanie, Linda and Michael. Chester was still born and Linda died of crib death. Helen would tell Jeanie and Michael that their dad's a hero. It wasn't until Michael was a grown man before he learned of his father's heroic efforts and bravery.

"I knew Dad had medals and he never said what he did," Michael said. "I started wearing them to school. I put them on my jacket and the kids would give me $5 for those medals. I started to think it was pretty neat that these people would buy my dad's medals. I was just in elementary school at the time when I was selling my dad's medals. He never got mad or upset about me selling the medals, but he was a disciplinarian when it came to competition."

"When I was growing up playing sports, I wondered why dad was so hard on me and my sister," Michael said. "I played baseball and basketball. Jeanie was in band and she played accordion, winning numerous music awards. She and dad traveled to state recitals across the country and even went to New York to make a record with her accordion group. Dad instilled in me and her that you always finish. Dad said, 'If I had quit, neither of you two would be here.' We had to be focused and strong minded to continue on with what we started."

"Not until I got in the military did I understand those are the medals you earn while you are in the service," Michael said. "After I told Dad I joined the military, he would tell me a few things that he went through as a prisoner of war under the Japanese. He didn't go into the cruelty, but he finally decided to let the generations know what went on. He decided to tell his story."

Many former prisoners of war never talked about their experiences, even up until their death beds. And, it would be 50 years before Phillip would talk about his experiences during the war and share his story of survival with his family, let alone the public. Phillip was a soldier in a particularly trying and little known period of American history. Even years after he left the military, his duty was to leave behind the true, unembellished story of his experiences during the war so future generations may learn from them.

Richard Gordon, a comrade in the 31st Infantry, urged Phillip to share his story because he was part of history. It was also at the encouragement of his former assistant gunner Ed Beyuka that Phillip started to talk about his time in the Pacific Theater. In 1993, Ed wrote Phillip asking about some of the experiences they went through.

Zuni, N.M.

Oct. 19, 1993

Dear Phil;

Just a short letter. Will write a long one next time. Hope you're in good health. I can't "spell" (words) correctly since it's been such a long time since I've written my letters.

Tell me some of the experiences we went thru together. At the "Mango Grove" when a dud fell to close and knocked me out. Who was the other comrade who helped you "drag" me to safety? Also of the "Lost Patrol," – not patrol but just LOST – when at about midnight you and I shared a can of sardines.

Perhaps thinking of the past is not for you, if that be the case, please forgive me & forget the questions. As for me it's good to talk about it & get it out.

I'll write or call again.

Sincerely –

Ed.

Phillip eventually became involved in a number of veteran organizations including the National Ex-Prisoners of War, Inc. (Korea, Pacific, Vietnam, and European Theater of Operations (ETO)), the American Defenders of Bataan and Corregidor, Inc., and the 31st Infantry Association, as well as the Battling Bastards of Bataan. He attended the annual conventions of these organizations and served as Secretary-Treasurer and Vice-Commander of the 31st Infantry Association. It was through his involvement with the 31st Infantry Association that he met other survivors from Company H. Until then, Phillip didn't have any idea of what happened to some of his buddies.

As Phillip began to share his story, he crisscrossed the country regularly for events and speaking engagements, talking about his heritage and his involvement in the military.

Although he was given much attention, he always remained humble. Over time, Phillip told his story of hope and perseverance, talking to veterans and young people in high school and college about overcoming adversity. He would share about the need to have a strong mind and continue on even when life and circumstances are hard. And, he always talked about how the Lord watched over him.

If anyone deserved to be depressed and bitter it would be Phillip, but he chose to pull himself by the bootstraps and keep going. He would walk into a room and was always so positive.

"One of the things I remember most was he kept saying, 'Don't give up. This Creek boy made it,'" said Daniel Wind III who brought Mr. Coon to speak to the Creek Nation Lighthorse Explorers Post 106, a group of aspiring boys and girls with an interest in law enforcement as a possible career.

"I remember very distinctly when Mr. Coon came into the room," said Daniel, Executive Officer with the Explorers. "It wasn't a big room, but there was a path in the room and he was in the back middle. I remember seeing him sitting there. He was telling us how hard the war was and how they were treated. He was blunt about it."

Phillip captivated everybody's attention at the Explorer's meeting.

"In our tradition, we honor our elders," Daniel said. "We honor them because they are elders, but when you know someone who has been through what Mr. Coon has been through you want to give them that much more respect because you've learned what he went through."

The Explorers Post would later accompany Phillip at veteran's events, often presenting the colors and representing the Muscogee (Creek) Nation.

"Wherever we traveled, when people saw dad's hat, which had an inscription about the Bataan Death March, they really wanted to talk to him," Michael said. "We would be eating out for dinner and dad never seemed to be able to finish a meal. People would come up to him and want their picture with him. He never seemed to mind."

When attending any veteran's event, Phillip wore his WWII gabardine uniform. It contained seven stripes, one for every six months he was held in captivity. Phillip was so proud of his uniform. He always stood straight and tall when he donned his uniform, as if he was being saluted. This was typical of former WWII POWs. They would stand tall and hold themselves well. They would stand straight even though it may hurt. They would show a lot of pride in themselves and for their service to the country. Their apparel, regardless of whether they were in blue jeans or suits, was sharp. Many would even press their blue jeans.[6]

Wherever he was, Phillip seemed to attract attention despite his humble stature. So many people wanted to take their picture with him. Phillip often joked, "It's only because I can still fit in my uniform."

On May 29, 2004, Phillip would especially be bombarded with requests for photos. That day the National World War II

Memorial was formally dedicated on the National Mall in Washington, D.C. It was a dedication Phillip didn't want to miss.

Accompanied by his wife Helen, son Michael, and grandson Robert, Phillip made the journey from his home in Sapulpa to the nation's capital to partake in the festivities. Located near the Lincoln Memorial and the Washington Monument, the National WWII Memorial serves as a point of gratitude from a thankful nation and a reminder to future generations of those who served their country during a very critical time. Phillip was a presence and had a presence about him wherever he went. Many visitors around the monument saw the military hat Phillip wore that day and began to ask him questions. He had a way of listening to people. Throughout the day, many people even had their pictures taken with him, saying it was an honor just to shake his hand.

1. Moyer, Moe. Interview by author. Taped interview. Norman, Oklahoma, November 2014.
2. Coffey.
3. Harrison.
4. Baldassarre.
5. Taryole.
6. Ibid, Moyer.

Phillip proudly reflects on the words of President Harry S Truman at the National Word War II Memorial, on the day of its dedication, Washington, D.C., May 29, 2004.

OUR DEBT TO THE HEROIC MEN AND VALIANT WOMEN IN THE SERVICE OF OUR COUNTRY CAN NEVER BE REPAID. THEY HAVE EARNED OUR UNDYING GRATITUDE. AMERICA WILL NEVER FORGET THEIR SACRIFICES.

PRESIDENT HARRY S TRUMAN

CHAPTER 24
RETURN TO THE PHILIPPINES

Later in life, Phillip would make it known that he held no resentment against the Japanese people. He was always at peace and one could see that in his eyes, despite the scars of war. He never carried a grudge and he lived in the present. He made peace with who he was and what happened to him.

"I don't have ill feelings over what happened to me because I made my choice," Phillip said, referring to his selection of going to the Philippines over Hawaii.

However, Phillip never had much desire to return to the place where they took his best friend from him. When presented with an opportunity to return to the Philippines, he said his heart wasn't in it.

One day Phillip's grandson Robert Coffey received an email from Major Richard Gordon requesting Phillip attend a cross dedication in the Philippines.

Richard was a staff sergeant when he and Phillip were on burial detail at Camp O'Donnell. Richard later retired as a major. In the early 1990s, Major Gordon was one of the founders of The Battling Bastards of Bataan, mostly comprised of members of the 31st Infantry. The group began with a newsletter called Chit Chat and from there it developed into a full-blown organization. The Battling Bastards of

Bataan were a close-knit group and only veterans could be members. Phillip attended the group's reunions and that's how he kept in contact with Major Gordon.[1]

"Grandpa never really wanted to go back and I relayed that message to Major Gordon," Robert said.

The Major was persistent and urged Phillip to reconsider as a replica of the Sack of Cement Cross was being built at Camp O'Donnell at the POW site. It was nearly 60 years after WWII that the family would hear the story of the Sack of Cement Cross.

"Your grandfather has to," Major Gordon wrote. "Your grandfather was one of a handful of individuals who built the Sack of Cement Cross."

"No one knew about the cross," Robert said. "Grandpa didn't mention it to anyone."[2]

Major Gordon was a driving force behind a monument to mark the death of approximately 1,600 Americans who died in Camp O'Donnell in a span of about 45 days. Major Gordon discussed with James Litton, a Battling Bastards of Bataan member who was living in Manila, about the possibility of building a monument in Camp O'Donnell. The monument is a large marble wall inscribed with the names of the deceased soldiers. Standing before the wall is a replica of the Sack of Cement Cross.

Phillip was the last survivor who worked on the Sack of Cement Cross and Major Gordon wanted him to help unveil the replica cross for the Camp O'Donnell Memorial Dedication honoring U.S. veterans. The dedication was held at Capas National Shrine on April 9, 2000.

Phillip agreed to go.

He was one of eight veterans to respond to the Rajah Tours invitation – three veterans who were on the Death March and five veterans from Corregidor. Relatives of those from both battles also responded to the tour invitation.[3]

Phillip, Helen, and Robert flew to San Francisco, where they had a long layover before flying to the Philippines. Upon arriving in Manila, Phillip remained silent at dinner and throughout the evening. When asked what was wrong, he said, "I miss my friend Jacob Cornsilk."

Phillip was reflective and there were many times he thought about Jacob on the trip.

Never thinking they would ever step foot back in the Philippines, the U.S. veterans from the 31st Infantry toured Manila, visiting the Walled City where they trained. The group went to Lipa where Phillip and other POWs had to make a runway for the Japanese Air Force.

"Someone had a map and grandpa was talking and showing everyone who was present how they built that airstrip," Robert said. "He never talked about the airstrip until that moment."

Prior to the unveiling ceremony of the replica cross at the Capas National Shrine, formerly known as Camp O'Donnell, the group went to Mariveles where the Death March started, and then on to Cabanatuan where they saw the POW camp. In Mariveles, Phillip was with one of the other travelers, a son of a Bataan survivor. They both looked up at the road which ascended up a steep incline of about 60 degrees, winding around the mountain, for about seven kilometers.

The son of the Bataan survivor asked Phillip, "How did you make it up this very steep climb?" Phillip looked at him and simply replied, "I was not given a choice."

As what has become tradition, a Filipino memorial is held on April 9. The ceremonies in 2000 then turned to the American memorial. The unveiling of the memorial was attended by U.S. Ambassador Thomas C. Hubbard and other dignitaries for a very formal ceremony. Phillip did the unveiling along with Major Gordon.

"The unveiling of the Sack of Cement Cross was historic to see," Robert said.[4]

The original Sack of Cement Cross remained hidden amidst tall cogon grass until it was discovered by returning American forces in 1945. Left where it originally stood, unknown to most, and battered by the elements, the cross was again forgotten.

"I remember the little cross we made out of a bag of cement. We had to mark the place where we buried our boys at that camp. I heard in 1953, from a nurse who had gone back over there, that the cross was still standing," Phillip said.

Rediscovered by Colonel John Olson, a Bataan veteran visiting the area in 1961, the cross became the historical symbol of the American prisoner of war enclosure and its dead.

When American military presence ended in the Philippines in 1992, the American Battle Monuments Commission brought the cross to the National Historic Site in Andersonville, Georgia, where it is now kept and displayed in a permanent place of honor. The original and a replica built in the Philippines stand as a reminder of America's unpreparedness before the outbreak of World War II.[5]

While Phillip was on his return trip to the Philippines, he met Tillman J. Rutledge, another veteran of the 31st Infantry who served in Company F, 2nd Battalion. They were both very happy to see each other, having become friends from reunions with the 31st Infantry Association. Both Philip and Tillman were on that Lipa, Batangas, work detail. Also part of the tour was another member of the 31st Infantry, Humphrey O'Leary. Humphrey lived in Manila with his wife and family.

While they were in the Philippines, a film production crew for BBC met the veterans at the Capas National Shrine. They were filming a documentary called, "Hell in the Pacific," a highly acclaimed four part documentary on WWII in the Pacific Theater. Unbeknownst to them, both Phillip and Tillman were to play a part in the documentary. They were filmed walking together, as they retraced their steps on part of the Death March trail. As they walked, they reminisced and recounted their experiences on that very lethal march.

Following the unveiling ceremony, the veterans then went to Corregidor.

"At Corregidor, there is a memorial for General MacArthur saying, 'I have returned.' Not one of those former prisoners of war got out to take pictures on the tour," Robert said. "A lot of people view MacArthur as a hero, but they, the former POWs, stayed on the bus. No one got out. The tour guide said, 'I will give you 10 minutes to get out and look around.' Not one got out. That's how grandfather felt. At that time, they had hard feelings. They felt like no one cared."

Although Phillip was an integral part of the cross' unveiling ceremony and monument dedication, his main reason to return was to see where Jacob was buried. Jacob was interred at the prisoner of war camp in O'Donnell and then transferred to Cabanatuan. His remains were then moved to one of the two temporary cemeteries in Manila, before being transferred to the Manila American Cemetery, in Makati, his final resting place.

Although Phillip didn't want to bring up all those bad memories, he was glad he went to the dedication. He lost so many of his friends and buddies in the Philippines, but when he got back home, Phillip said he was glad he had the opportunity to honor his fallen comrades.

1. Baldassarre.
2. Coffey.
3. "Outline of Events."
4. Coffey.
5. National Prisoner of War Museum.

Phillip returns to the Philippines for the Camp O'Donnell Memorial Dedication at Capas National Shrine on April 9, 2000.

Phillip stands next to the KM1 Death March Marker on his return visit to the Philippines.

CHAPTER 25
THE RIDE HOME

In 2007, Phillip learned about The Ride Home, a retreat dedicated to honoring all former Prisoners of War and remembering those still Missing in Action. With Helen urging him to attend, Phillip decided he wanted to go to the retreat which is held annually in Andersonville, Georgia.

Former Prisoners of War and family members of the Missing in Action gather annually in September for memorial tributes, recognition ceremonies, and medal presentations – sometimes long overdue medal presentations. There are also lectures, for instance, about scientific advances in identifying those Missing in Action.

"One of the things you'd observe (at the retreat) as you walk by two, three, four men who were incarcerated by the enemy of a country, beaten, tortured, starved to death almost, would be chuckling between the POWS as they sit reminiscing," said Moe Moyer, chairman of the board for The Ride Home. "And as tragic as Phillip's story is, there was always a smile on his face. He had a tendency to make the most of it. He took the positive out of it and he was a better man for it."

John Harrison, one of the original event organizers, was well aware of the fact that Phillip was a Bataan Death March survivor and wanted to introduce him to someone special when he arrived at The Ride Home.

"I want you to meet someone," John said to Phillip as he took him to meet another Death March survivor.

As soon as Phillip and the other survivor were within 10 feet of each other they instantly recognized one another nearly 65 years later.

"I know him," Phillip said to John. "I used to follow behind him on the march because he was tall and blocked the sun."

"I thought he was a Jap because of his dark skin," said the other survivor, who like so many on the march wouldn't turn around to see who was behind them for fear of retaliation.

John recalled that the two were both shocked to see each other. "They talked about the Death March and the severe mistreatment by the Japanese," John said. "They talked about the hellships. They were on the same ship, but they didn't see each other on the ship. Phillip shared about how upset he was that some of those ships were sunk by U.S. submarines. They talked about friends lost in the Philippines and friends they made while in the service."[1]

At The Ride Home, Phillip also recognized fellow Bataan Death March survivor John Mims, who was in Company B, 31st Infantry Regiment. The two trained at Fort William McKinley at the same time. "In my opinion he was just a good, super guy," Mims said of Phillip. "He had a heart of gold." John now makes his home in Aberdeen, North Carolina, and he travels the country, lecturing about his WWII experience in order to keep the memory of Bataan alive.[2]

During The Ride Home, a "Never Forget" ceremony is held at the National Historic Site at Andersonville, Georgia, home of the National Prisoners of War Museum.

Following each ceremony, Phillip would often be found in the Prisoner of War Museum, where the Sack of Cement Cross now has a permanent home. The cross stands in a dark room, reflective of the dark days in the Philippines. Phillip often shared first-hand with visitors about the cross. It was as if he was holding court at the cross, providing a living history lesson to a packed room of visitors about how this memorial was built and its significance.

"Dad knew the cross was here and he told me I had to come see something," Michael said. "It was an amazing feeling to see what my dad did."

"When Mr. Coon came to his first Ride Home, he would stand to the side or he would stand to the back of the room at the events," Moe said. "Mr. Coon soon became his own little star. He was a hoot with all the second generation POWs – from Korea and Vietnam both – and they would be engaged by him. In a sense they were brothers, whether they were Korean or Vietnam POWs, they had respect for him because of what he went through. And, at some point during the evening, the entire attention would focus on Mr. Coon."

Helen would always accompany Phillip to The Ride Home. She loved to sing and before one of the candlelight ceremonies, she sang "Amazing Grace." Shy in her own right, when Helen performed she charmed her audiences with her heartwarming presence. One could literally hear a pin drop in the auditorium when she sang. "Amazing Grace" is such a somber song, but the applause following her performance was deafening. Year after year, veterans would ask if she was going to sing again.

"I have nothing but sheer respect and honor for Mr. Coon," Moe said. "The man just blew me away with his peace and calm after all he had been through in his life, both militarily and personally. I hope I can work on being the type of man he was. He had the right stuff. It was always a treat to be in his presence, as well as Helen's."[3]

1.   John Harrison.
2.   Mims, John. Interview by author. Personal interview. Americus, Georgia, September 2014.
3.   Moyer.

CHAPTER 26
JAPAN 70 YEARS LATER

Phillip was liberated September 19, 1945. But he would say he was liberated before that from something greater than the POW camps. He was liberated from sin through Jesus Christ. He was not only a soldier for this country, but he was a soldier for the cross. And, this true liberation would allow Phillip to ultimately forgive the enemy who stole his youth.

Nearly 70 years after WWII, Phillip returned to Japan. He and Michael, along with three other former POWs and three widows of POWs, were invited by the Government of Japan to participate in the fourth Japanese/American POW Friendship Program. Started in 2010 under the Democratic Party of Japan administration led by Yukio Hatoyama, The Friendship Program seeks to promote mutual understanding between the Japanese and American people.

Under the backdrop of a dark blue morning sky and escorted by Rolling Thunder, Inc., a nonprofit organization dedicated to raising awareness of POW/MIA issues, Phillip and Michael left the Sapulpa Indian Community Center on October 12, 2013, and headed toward the Tulsa International Airport for their flight to Tokyo, Japan.

The Rolling Thunder Oklahoma Chapter 1 often escorted Phillip to veteran's events. "We love Mr. Coon," said John Lehmann, Rolling Thunder local chapter vice president. "When Michael asked us to be there, there was no question. He's already part of the family and we'll be there when he comes home."

Phillip and Michael arrived in Japan on October 13. Along with the other veterans, they started their nine-day tour by visiting the Commonwealth War Cemetery in Yokohama where the ashes of 48 American POWs are enshrined in the Memorial Hall.

The veterans met with Japanese Foreign Minister Fumio Kishida, who thanked the POW delegation for accepting his government's invitation to visit Japan. He reiterated Japan's heartfelt apology for inhumane treatment and sufferings they experienced during WWII as prisoners of war of the Japanese. He also expressed his hope that this visit would promote further reconciliation and wished the delegation a fruitful stay in Japan.

The American delegation attended a luncheon hosted by Mr. Koji Tomita, Director General, North American Affairs Bureau. The delegation was later the center of attention at a press conference by the National Press Club, where Phillip presented a Muscogee (Creek) robe to the press club. They also conducted a public lecture at Temple University, Japan Campus, providing testimony of their experiences during the war. The group then visited the U.S. Embassy, where Phillip left a Muscogee (Creek) Nation tribal shawl for Ambassador Caroline Kennedy. As a result of his gift, Phillip received this letter from Ambassador Kennedy.

AMBASSADOR OF
THE UNITED STATES OF AMERICA
TOKYO

February 28, 2014

Mr. Phillip Coon
13162 South Maple Street
Glenpool, OK 74033

Dear Mr. Coon,

Thank you very much for the beautiful Muscogee tribal shawl. I am deeply
honored to receive this gift.

My colleagues informed me about your tribulations after being captured by
the Japanese in 1942, including being forced to endure the Bataan Death March
and suffering in Japanese POW camps. I can't begin to imagine your hardship, but
I am truly impressed by your willingness to confront this ordeal, including your
participation in the Japanese-American POW Friendship Program. It takes
enormous strength to overcome past transgressions, but even more courage to
forgive. Your visit to Japan, as part of a reconciliation program led by the
Japanese government, is a true testament to our strong friendship with the people
of Japan.

You are inspiring, Mr. Coon, thank you for your service to our country.

Sincerely,

Caroline Kennedy

At a reception hosted by Parliamentary Vice-Foreign Minister Hirotaka Ishihara, Michael presented a Muscogee (Creek) robe to Minister Ishihara as a gift from his father and the tribe.

The American veterans also visited their respective sites where they were held as prisoners of war. Phillip, Michael, Mr. Erwin Johnson, his wife Ann, and Mrs. Esther Jennings visited the former site of the Kosaka POW camp. While at

Kosaka, Phillip presented Mayor Hosokoshi with a 75-pound granite memorial plaque displaying his unit, assignment, and prisoner of war status as slave labor at the copper mine. According to Mayor Hosokoshi, the memorial will be on permanent display at the Kosaka Mine Office.

"Around 15:00, October 17, in 2013, I had the honor of meeting Mr. Phillip Coon and an attendant from the Ministry of Foreign Affairs, at the old local government office," Mayor Hosokoshi wrote in a letter regarding Mr. Coon's biography. "After we greeted each other, I noticed the medal, which he gave to me, was especially made for his visit to Japan. This fact proves how he was respected as a human treasure representing the Mascogy [sic] Creek people."

"I was born after the war, in 1947, and grew up in Kosaka; however, I have scarcely had chance to enter the Kosaka Mining, and do not know how the lives of the POWs in those days had been," the Mayor continued. "In Kosaka, we have preserved the buildings of those days, when Mr. Coon was held here as a POW, as the legacy of the modernization, and they are still used. I wonder what he felt seeing them, which makes me feel pains in my heart."

Following trips to the respective POWS camps, the entire delegation visited Kyoto, where the name cards of 48,000 Allied soldiers who died on Japanese territory are kept in the Memorial Hall of this temple. They also visited Ritsumeikan University's Kyoto Museum for World Peace. Phillip presented a Muscogee robe, ball sticks, turtle rattle, and ribbon shirt to the museum. These items are now on permanent display at the museum in memory of Phillip W. Coon.[1]

During their trip, the American POW delegation intended to

improve relations and a path for reconciliation with victims, promoting understanding and healing. For Phillip, the trip provided closure for his time at war. Seventy years later, Phillip came full circle with forgiveness for the Japanese people.

On the evening of October 21, 2013 Phillip returned home from Japan to a hero's welcome from fellow veterans, the Rolling Thunder, and well-wishers. Phillip was humbled by the reception and his quick wit was priceless.

When asked about Japan, Phillip answered, "It is still there. This time I got a lot more to eat than I did the first time."[2]

1.   Website source: Japanese/American POW Friendship Program.
2.   *Muscogee Nation News.*

Phillip Coon (left) presents a memorial granite plaque to Mayor Hosokoshi of Kosaka, Japan. According to the mayor, the plaque will be on permanent display at the Kosaka Mine Office in remembrance of Phillip's time as a POW.

CHAPTER 27
LASTING LEGACY

For service to his country, Phillip W. Coon received the American Defense Service Ribbon with one Bronze Star, an Asiatic Pacific Campaign Ribbon with two Bronze Stars, the Philippine Defense Ribbon with one Bronze Star, a Distinguished Unit Badge with two Oak Leaf Clusters, and the prized "Combat Infantry Badge," given only to soldiers who battled in the front lines. After 70 years, Phillip finally received the Prisoner of War Medal. U.S. Army Major General Rita Aragon, Oklahoma's Secretary of Veterans Affairs, presented the long-overdue medal to Phillip upon his 2013 return trip from Japan.[1]

In June 1979, he received the Cross of Valor from the Oklahoma Department of Veterans Affairs, which is the highest award that the state bestows to war veterans who reside in Oklahoma.

In 2009, he was presented a Prisoner of War Medallion of Honor from The Rolling Thunder on its cross country Flame of Freedom Ride. The Rolling Thunder stopped in Okmulgee, Oklahoma, and presented the Medallion of Honor to Phillip before the Muscogee (Creek) Nation National Council.

Phillip was chosen as the Grand Marshall for the Gila River Indian Community parade in Arizona in March 2012 commemorating Ira Hayes, who was part of the historic flag raising by U.S. Marines on Mt. Suribachi in Iwo Jima, as captured in the famous photograph by Joe Rosenthal.

In April 2014, the Quilts of Honor Foundation presented Mr. Coon with the Quilt of Valor. It was presented by quilt maker Sarah Wheatley, Daughters of the American Revolution.

Phillip was a great Native American among "The Greatest Generation." He was so very proud of his Creek heritage and proud of serving his country. He was equally proud of other Native Americans serving the country, especially his son, Michael, and grandson, Michael Keith.

Phillip's son Michael Coon signed up for voluntary duty during the Vietnam era, enlisting in the Army on February 26, 1971. He did his Basic Combat Training and Advanced Individual Training at Fort Leonard Wood in Missouri. He aspired to be in an airborne unit and went to Fort Benning, Georgia. Then he was transferred to Fort Bragg in North Carolina. He was with the 82nd Airborne Division for about a week before receiving orders to go to the Republic of Vietnam (South Vietnam) as a clerk. By the time Michael went home to take care of his affairs, the Army had changed his orders and he stayed at Fort Bragg Headquarters Company, working on the general's staff, HHC 18th Airborne Corp G2 Section. A former Army paratrooper, Michael served until December 1973.

"I had orders to go to Vietnam, and at the last minute they changed my orders. They put me on the general staff, and dad was proud of me," Michael said. "Dad told me, 'Son, you just have to take what the Army deals you. Everything happens for a reason and maybe they figured we endured enough with the family.'"

"I just wanted to have a good military record like dad did," Michael said. "Nobody filled his shoes, but he always told me, 'You fulfilled your mission in life of being a soldier.'"

Phillip's grandson Michael Keith Coon joined the Army at age 23 in 2005. He completed his Basic Combat Training at Fort Benning and transferred to Camp Irwin in California. Michael Keith was then sent to Fort Riley in Kansas. While at Fort Riley, he was deployed to Iraq from 2009 to 2010 and Afghanistan from 2011 to 2012. He was a .50 caliber gunner, a fire team leader, a weapons squad leader, and now serves as a platoon sergeant with Alpha Company 177 AR at Fort Bliss, Texas. Michael Keith's next tour of duty will likely be to Eastern Africa.

"I joined because of how my grandfather put boots on the ground," Michael Keith said. "Hopefully, we will keep the line going and hopefully one of my sons will continue the legacy my grandfather started." [2]

Phillip no doubt left a legacy that would serve his country, and the Lord, for years to come. Phillip always wanted others to know, in spite of the horrors and tribulations he faced, "This Creek boy made it!"

He made it because of the Muscogee (Creek) ancestors who had gone before him, the trust and friendship of four Army buddies, and faith in silent prayer. Phillip made it because of several strong women in his life including his mother, grandmother, sister Sophie, daughter Jeanie, wife Helen and mother-in-law Fenie Simmer. Phillip and Sophie continued their close sibling connection as Sophie even took care Phillip's son Michael for awhile when Helen was ill. Fenie would also lend a helping hand, raising Michael until Helen was released from the hospital. Jeanie would always be "daddy's little girl," even long after she married. However on April 19, 1982, nothing could have prepared Phillip for the day Jeanie's life was tragically taken as a result of a school shooting where she worked. He would miss his daughter dearly. He would equally miss his sweet Helen as she passed away in March 2013, after 67 years of marriage.

On June 23, 2014 Phillip W. Coon departed on his final journey, joining his Lord, loved ones and his precious wife after serving them with sustaining love.

1. Gerald Wofford, "WWII veteran makes historic trip," *Muscogee Nation News.*

2. Wofford, "Creek Veteran Travels to Asia to Honor Fallen."

Phillip longs for his late wife, Helen, as he sits near her gravesite at the Fort Gibson National Cemetery in Oklahoma.

Funeral processional with Phillip's casket, draped with honor.

THE WHITE HOUSE

WASHINGTON

August 4, 2014

The Family of Phillip Coon
Glenpool, Oklahoma

Dear Coon Family:

    I was deeply saddened to learn of Phillip's passing, and I extend my heartfelt condolences as you mourn his loss and reflect upon his life.

    A selfless patriot, Phillip fought to advance the cause of freedom in the Pacific and helped change the course of an entire century. He showed the courage and strength to persevere in the face of tremendous adversity, and our Nation is forever indebted to him and all former prisoners of war who sacrificed their liberty to secure our own. Phillip touched lives across his community as a respected elder, and while he will be dearly missed, I trust his spirit will live on in the hearts of those who knew and loved him.

    May fond memories help temper your grief, and may you find comfort in one another's presence. Please know you will remain in my thoughts and prayers.

Sincerely,

In August 2014, the Coon family received this letter from President Barack Obama.

A Soldier's Silent Prayer

*A collection of personal memorabilia and photography
celebrating the life and times of Phillip W. Coon*

*Phillip's
Army khaki
uniform
and Muscogee
(Creek) Nation
vest.*

His field mess kit.

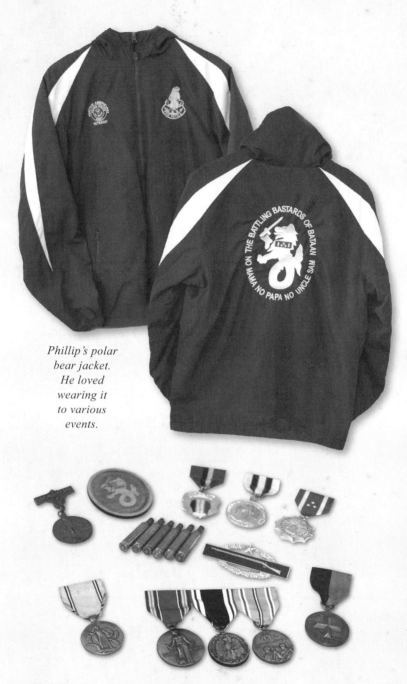

Phillip's polar bear jacket. He loved wearing it to various events.

Medals and medallions awarded to Phillip during his service to the United States. The spent shells are part of his 21-gun salute.

1937 Okemah Baseball Team (Phillip is in the top row, third from the left).

Haskell Baseball Team (Phillip is in the bottom row, fourth from the left).

Phillip lettered in baseball at Haskell Institute from 1939 to 1941.

Phillip poses for a shot on the field of Haskell Stadium.

The veteran returns for a visit to Haskell Institute in 1947.

Phillip's high school portrait (above). Outside the dorms at Haskell Institute (right).

Students at Euchee Boarding School in the early 1900s.

Photos courtesy: Sapulpa Historical Society.

Phillip's freshman class at Euchee Boarding School (middle row, right).

There were several strong women who were very important in Phillip's life: his wife, Helen Simmer (left) and his mother, Missaley Johnson Coon (below).

Pictured below, from left: Phillip's mother-in-law, Fenie Simmer; sister, Sophie Taryole; and, wife, Helen Simmer.

Phillip's lifelong friend, Ed Beyuka, with his rifle during premarksmanship training.

Ed sends a letter to his friend, Phillip, nearly 50 years after the end of the war and reflects on his memories of their time during battle, and how Phillip saved his life.

Zuni, N. M.
Oct. 19, 1993.

Dear Phil,

Just a short letter. Will write a long one next time.

Hope you're in good health. I can't "spell" (words) correctly since it's been such a long time since I've written any letters.

Tell me some of the experiences we went thru together. At the "Mango Grove" when a shell fell too close & knocked one out. Who was the other comrade who helped you "drag" me to safety? Also of the "Lost Patrol,"—not patrol but just LOST— when at about midnight you and I shared a can of sardines.

Perhaps thinking of the past is not for you, — if that be the case, please forgive me & forget the questions. As for me it's good to talk about it & get it out.

I'll write or call again.

Sincerely,
Ed.

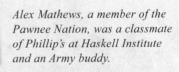

Alex Mathews, a member of the Pawnee Nation, was a classmate of Phillip's at Haskell Institute and an Army buddy.

Phillip and an Army buddy
become the stars on a postcard
sent from Fort Bliss, Texas
on February 11, 1946
to Phillip's family in Okemah.

At the White House, President Truman announces Japan's surrender.
Abbie Rowe, Washington, DC, August 14, 1945.

"F4U's and F6F's fly in formation during surrender ceremonies;
Tokyo, Japan. USS Missouri, left foreground."

Photos courtesy: National Archives & Records Administration

"Gen. Douglas MacArthur signs as Supreme Allied Commander during formal surrender ceremonies on the USS Missouri in Tokyo Bay. Behind Gen. MacArthur are Lt. Gen. Jonathan Wainright and Lt. Gen. A. E. Percival." Lt. C.F. Wheeler, September 2, 1945.

Instrument Of Surrender Of The Japanese Armed Forces And Related Documents ("Japanese Surrender Documents"), 1945.

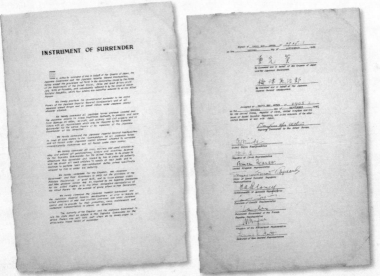

Photos courtesy: National Archives & Records Administration

Michael Coon, Phillip's son, locates the inscription of his dad's best friend, Jacob Cornsilk, on the Camp O'Donnell Monument at the Capas National Shrine in Capas, Tarlac; a closeup of his name below.

The 1936 Chilocco boxing team. Phillip's buddy, Jacob Cornsilk, attended Chilocco Indian Agricultural School and was a member of the boxing team.

CHILOCCOAN

BOXING TEAM — 1936

"The Chiloccoan" High School yearbook from 1936 and 1938.

In 2005, Phillip was inducted into the Haskell Hall of Fame for his outstanding athletic ability in baseball and basketball. During the ceremony, he was honored with a POW MIA plaque. Phillip always wore his uniform to any ceremony or veterans formal event.

Phillip poses with fellow 2005 Haskell Hall of Fame inductees.

Former Euchee Boarding School students dedicate a
historical marker where the school once stood in Sapulpa,
Oklahoma. Phillip attended Euchee as a young boy.

Phillip participates in the Euchee Boarding School monument dedication. The Seminole Nation Honor Guard accompany Phillip at the ceremony.

The tradition of honor and service is carried from father to son. Phillip and his son, Michael, proudly served in the U.S. Army.

Phillip is pictured with Simon Harry (to his right) and the Muscogee (Creek) Nation Honor Guard, before being recognized at a Tulsa Driller's baseball game in 2014, when he received the Quilt of Valor.

Phillip and his grandson, Robert Coffey, at the Black Creek Gourd Society Annual Gourd Dance in 2010 at the U.S. Navy Memorial Plaza in Washington, DC.

Phillip shakes hands with Navajo Code Talkers at the Gourd Dance.

Phillip stands near the Sack of Cement Cross at the National Prisoner of War Museum in Andersonville, Georgia (above), and admires a portrait of his life that is on display in Andersonville (below). Phillip is pictured with former museum superintendent, Brad Bennett.

Phillip honored by the State House of Representatives.

Oklahoma State Rep. Mark McCullough (R), District 30, recognizes Phillip W. Coon on April 11, 2011 as "Veteran of the Week." Rep. McCullough (left) and Muscogee (Creek) Nation Chief George Tiger (right) applaud Phillip's heroics.

Phillip honored as "Veteran of the Week."

Photo by Gerald Wofford; courtesy of Mvskoke Media

Phillip was honored with a salute during Veteran's Night at the Women's World College Softball Series in Oklahoma City in 2013.

Photo courtesy of Mvskoke Media

Phillip with his beloved wife, Helen.

Four former POWs of the
Japanese and three widows
of POWs were invited by the
government of Japan for the
2013 Japanese/American
POW Friendship Program.

Phillip is escorted onto the
grounds of the Yokohama
Cremation Memorial for a
commemorative photo.

Hirotaka Ishihara
Parliamentary Vice-Minister for Foreign Affairs
requests the pleasure of the company of
Mr. Phillip Coon and Mr. Michael Dennis Coon
at a reception of the Japanese/POW Friendship Program
Wednesday, October 16, 2013 from 18:30 to 20:30
at Saga, Sheraton Miyako Hotel Tokyo
1-1-50 Shirokanedai, Minato-ku, Tokyo

Contact: Yujiro Hayashi (Takafumi Iwasaki, Yuki Wakasugi) Tel. 03-5501-8276
First North America Division, North American Affairs Bureau, MOFA
*Please bring this card with you

Phillip and his son,
Michael, were honored
guests at the reception
in Shirokanedai,
Minato-ku, Tokyo
on October 16, 2013.

Phillip and his son, Michael, at the World Peace Museum with Professor Kazuyo Yamane.

As part of the 2013 Japanese/American Friendship Tour, POWs visit with Foreign Minister Fumio Kishida.

Friendship Meeting sponsored by the Japanese Society for Friendship with ex-POWS and their families.

フィリップ・クーン

Phillip Coon poses outside the Kosaka Mine Office on his return trip to Japan in 2013.

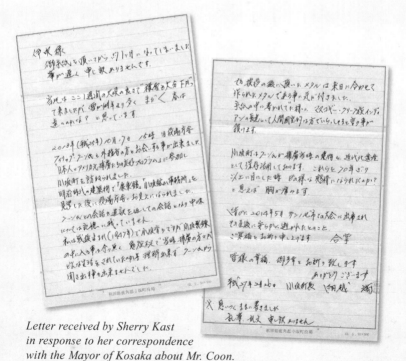

Letter received by Sherry Kast in response to her correspondence with the Mayor of Kosaka about Mr. Coon.

*From youthful recruit to decorated
U.S. soldier, Phillip was proud
to serve his family, friends,
comrades, heritage, country and,
ultimately, his Lord and Savior.*

*Beloved by his wife,
children, and family,
respected by his tribe,
and honored by his
country, the memory
and legacy of Phillip
W. Coon will live
long in the annals
of history and the
stories of generations
to come.*

*In this most
memorable photo,
Phillip proudly wears
"The Quilt of Valor".*